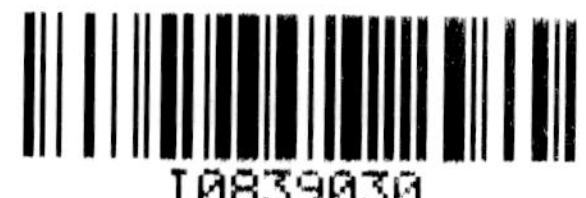


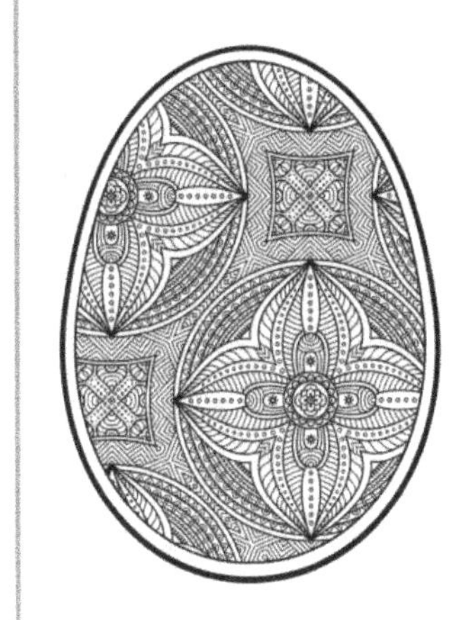
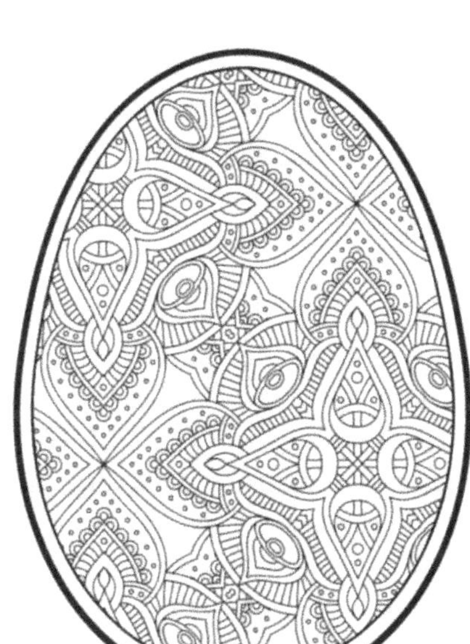
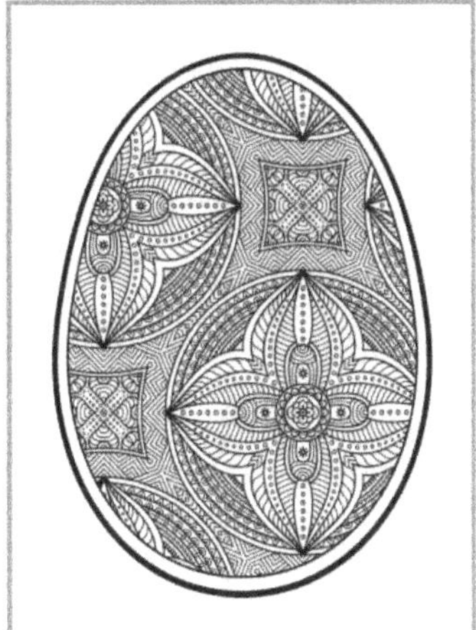
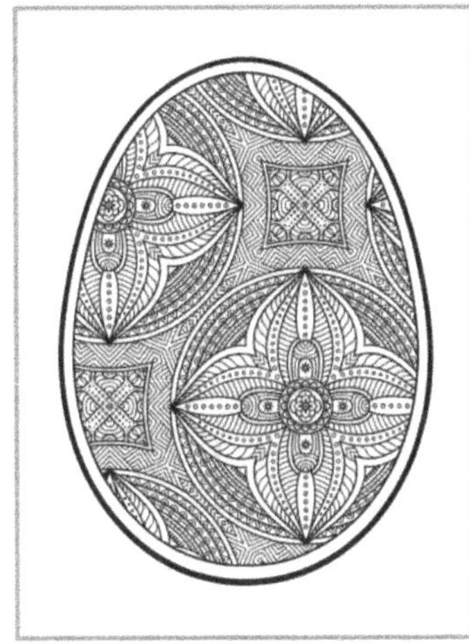
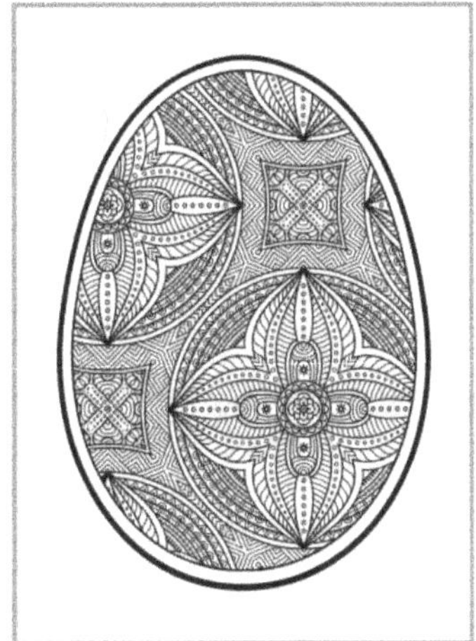

# THIS BOOK BELONGS TO

# COLOR TESTING PAGE

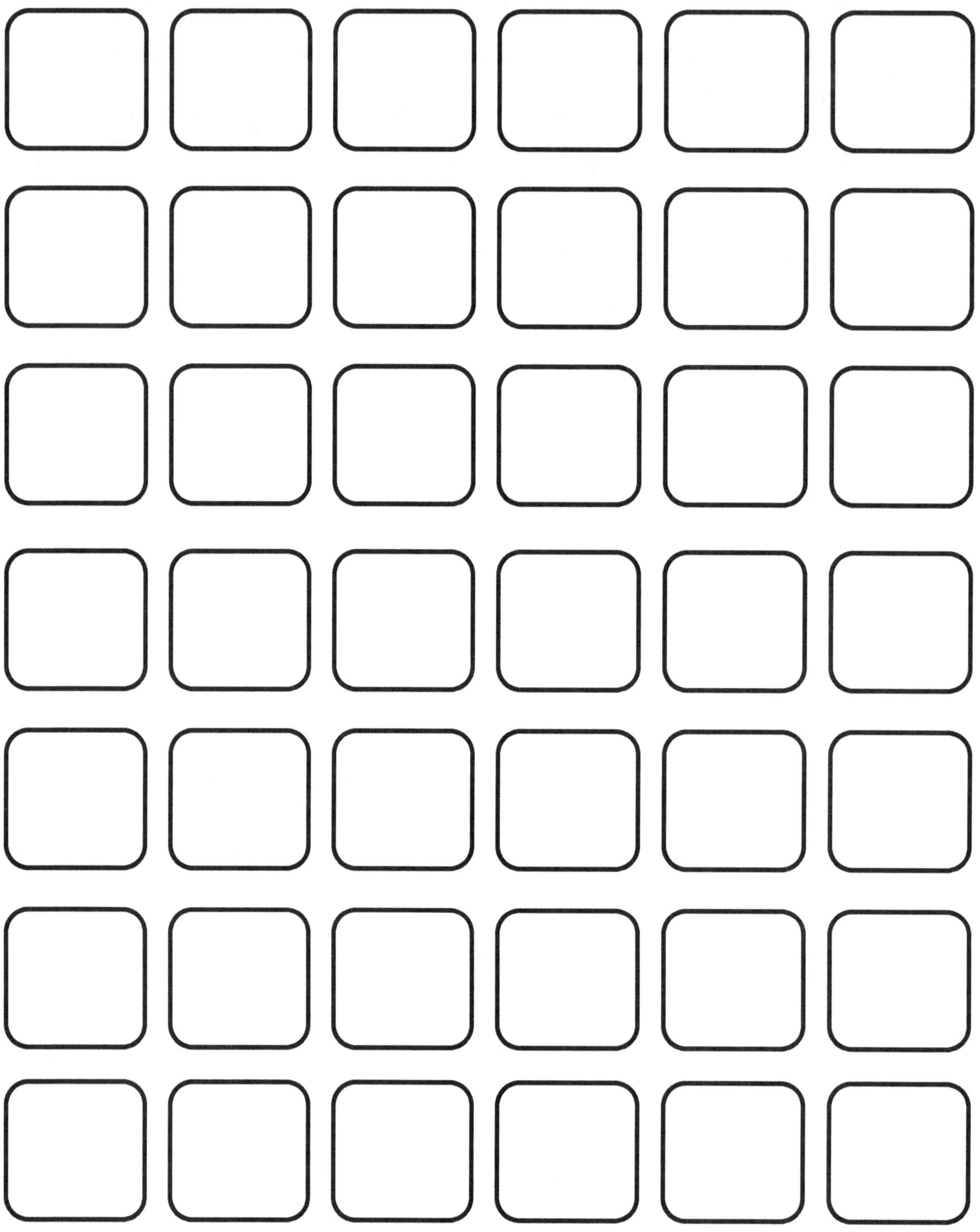

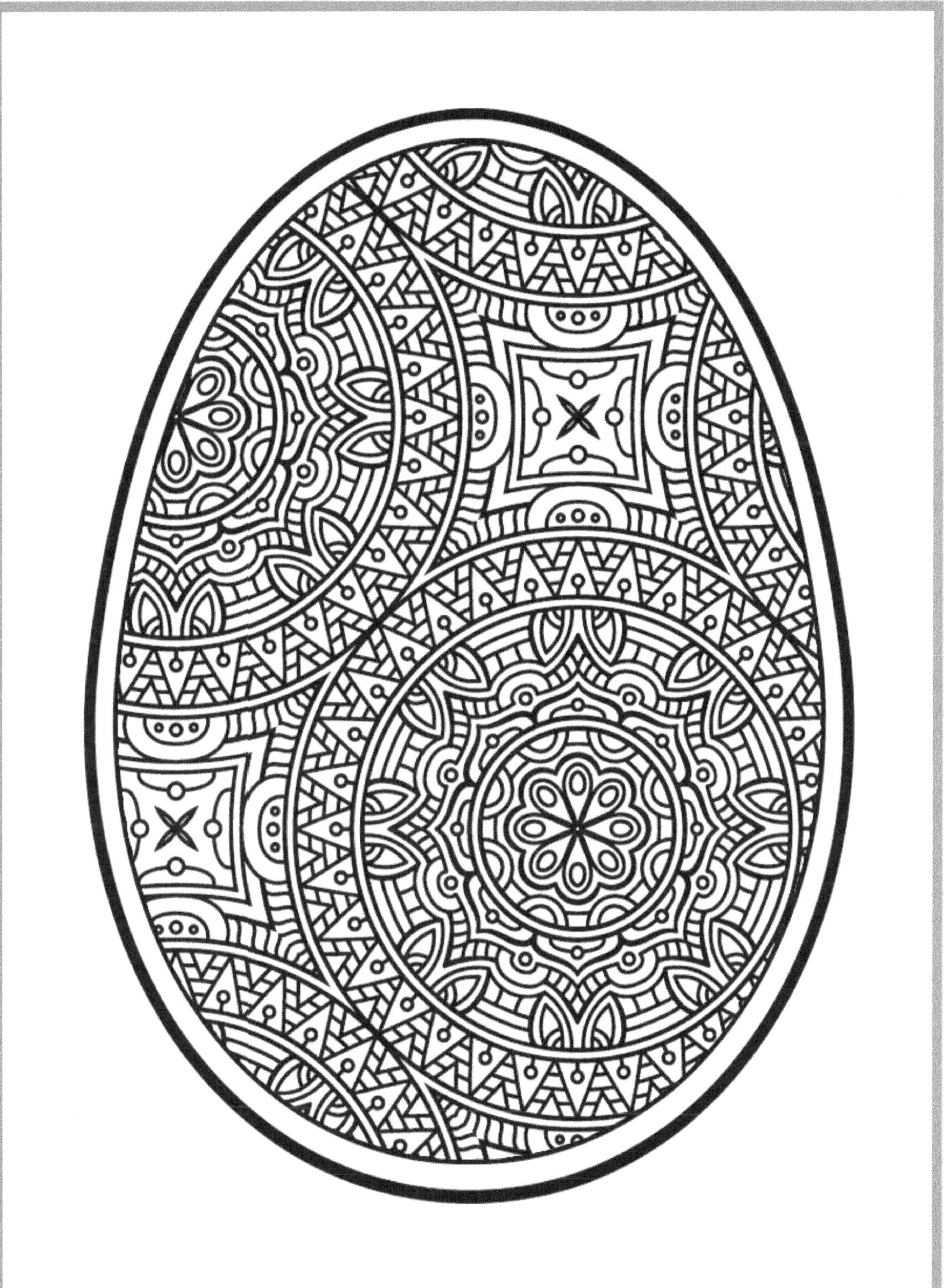

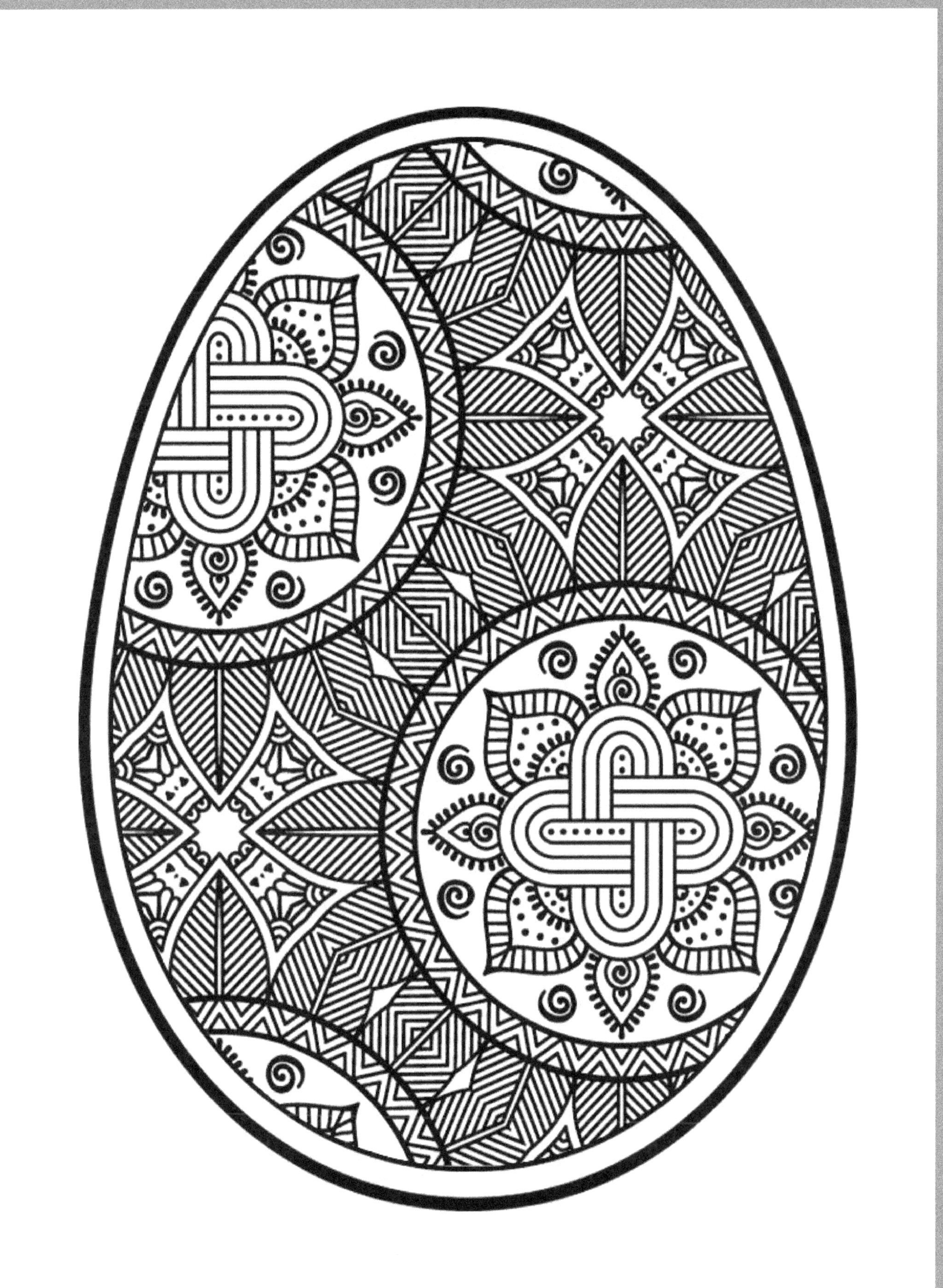

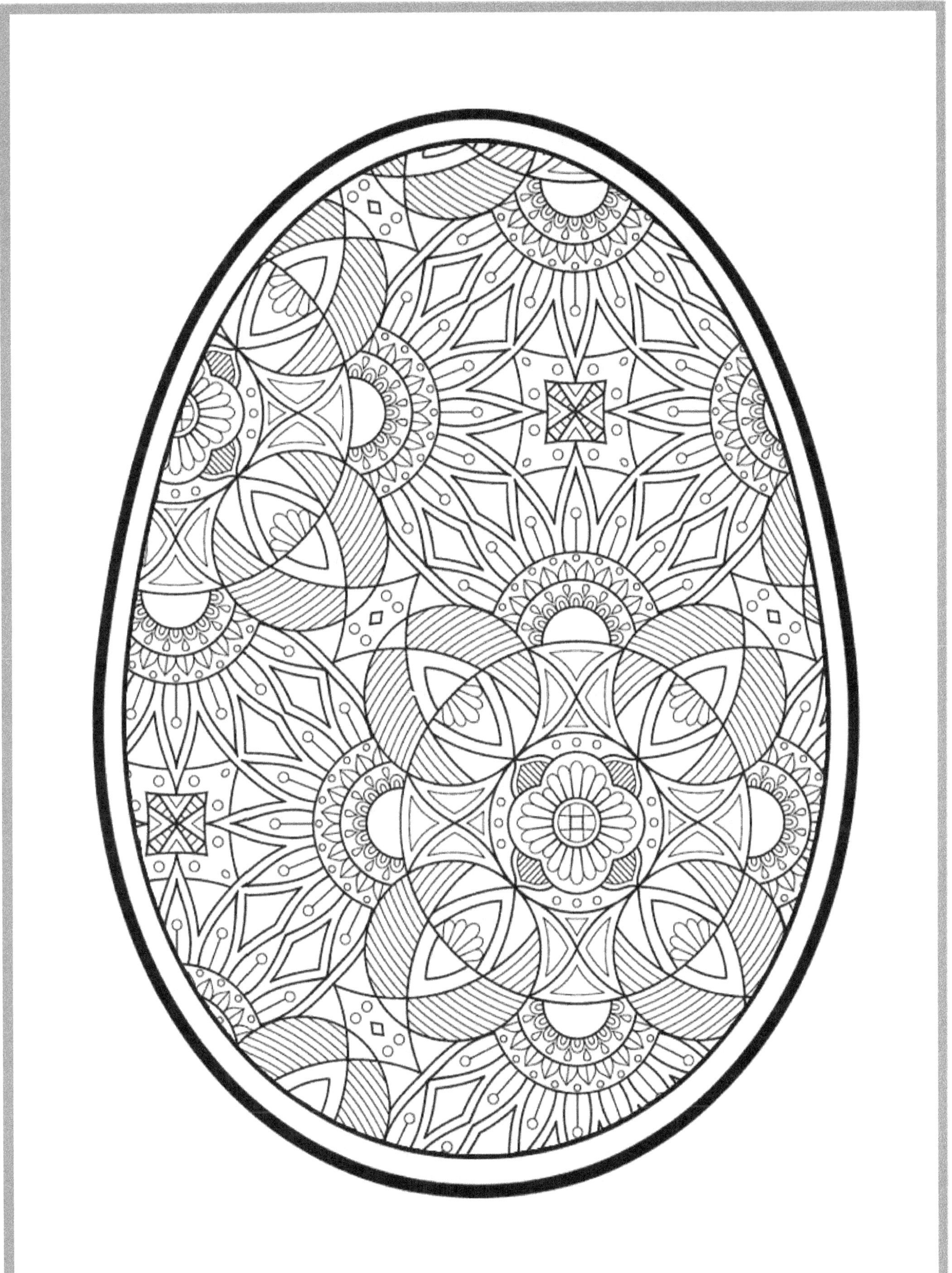

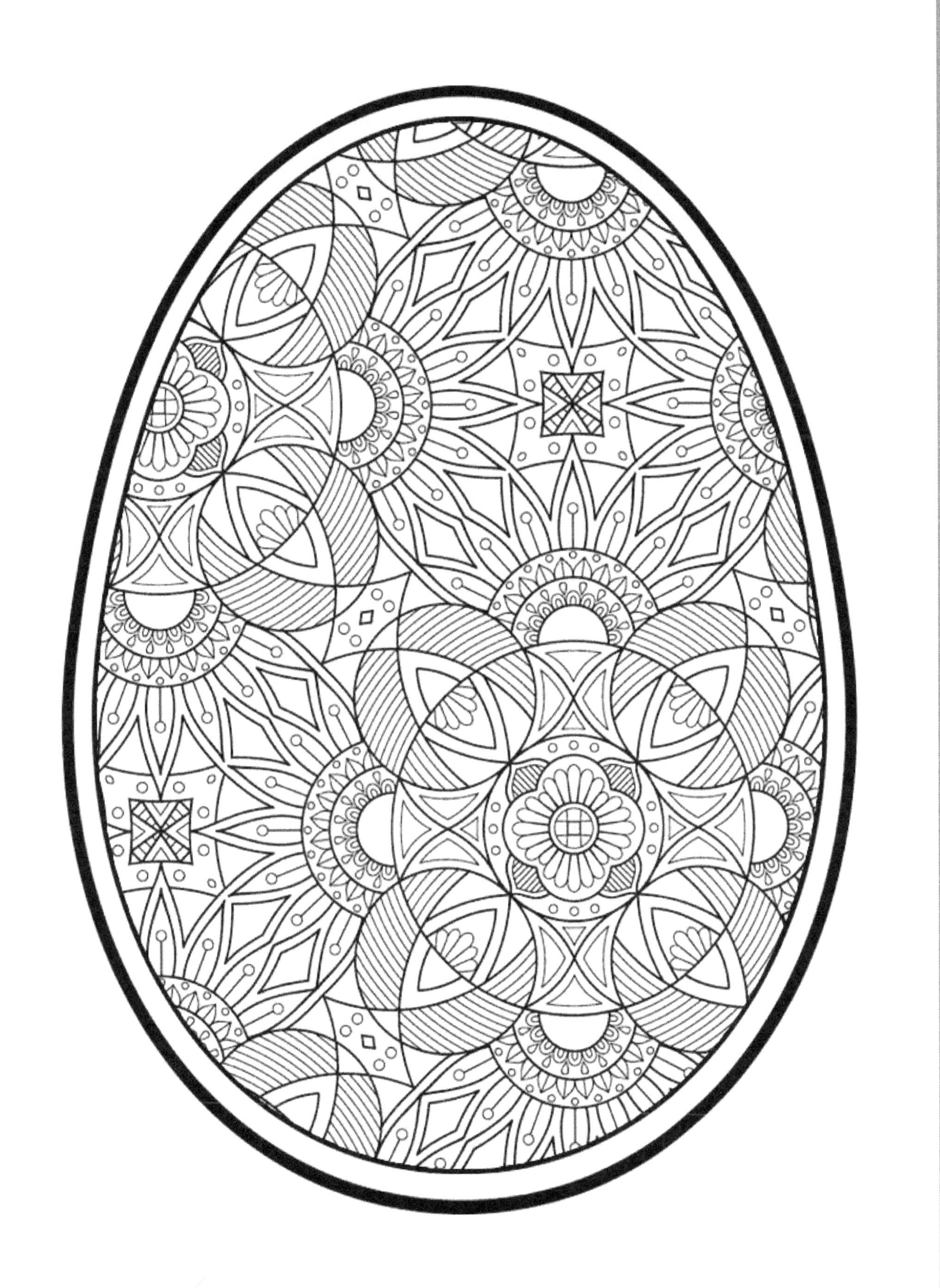

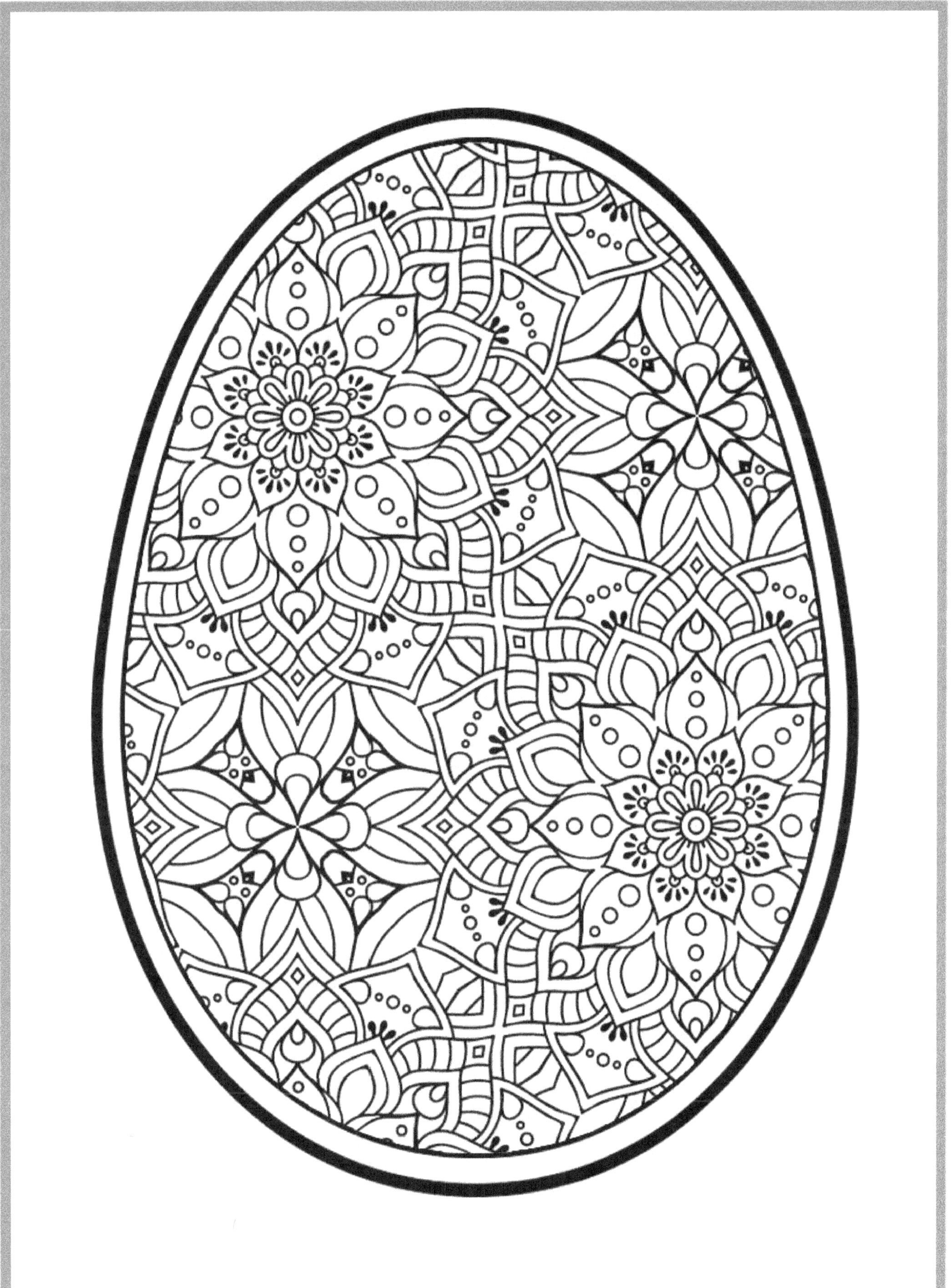

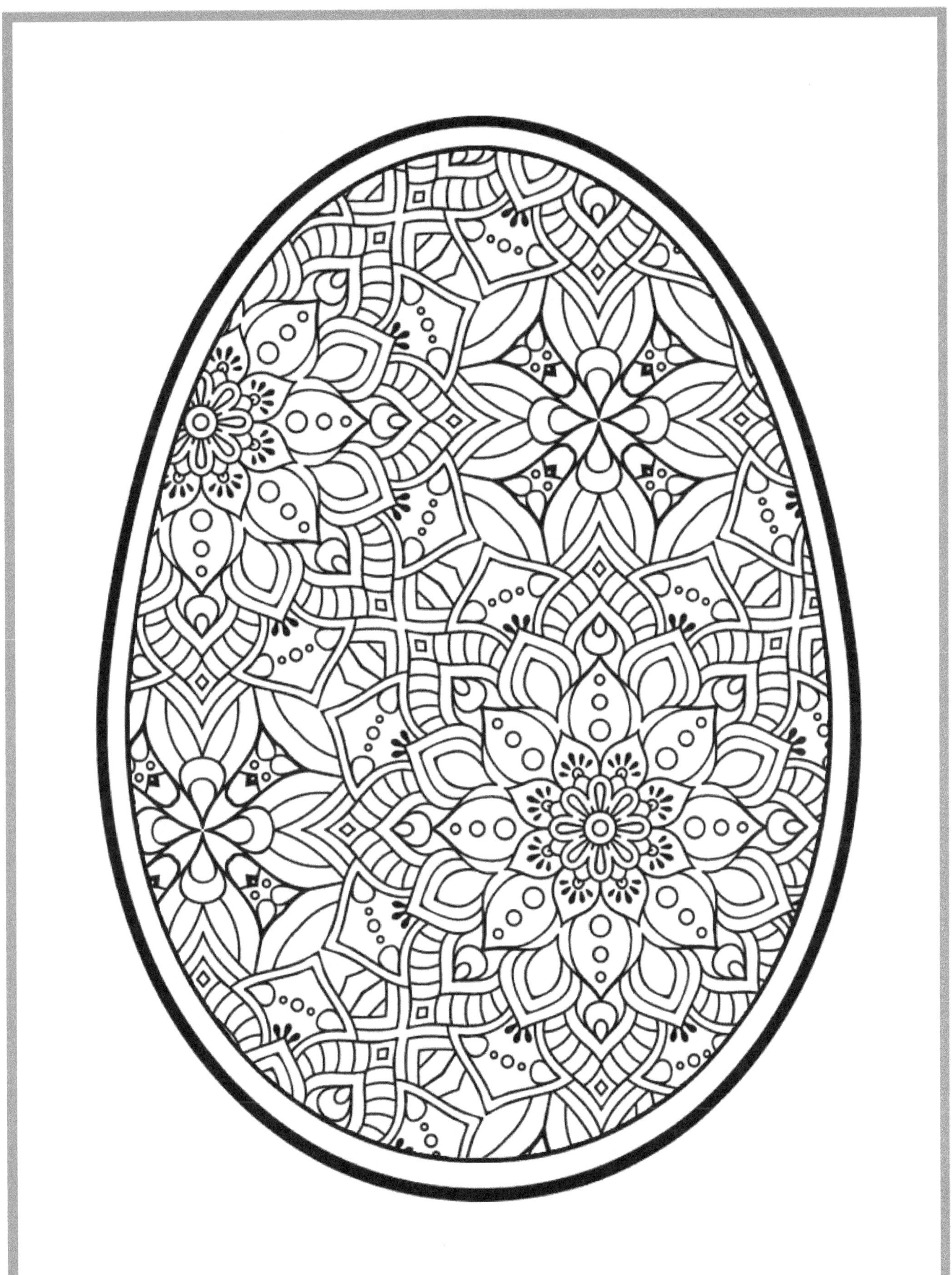

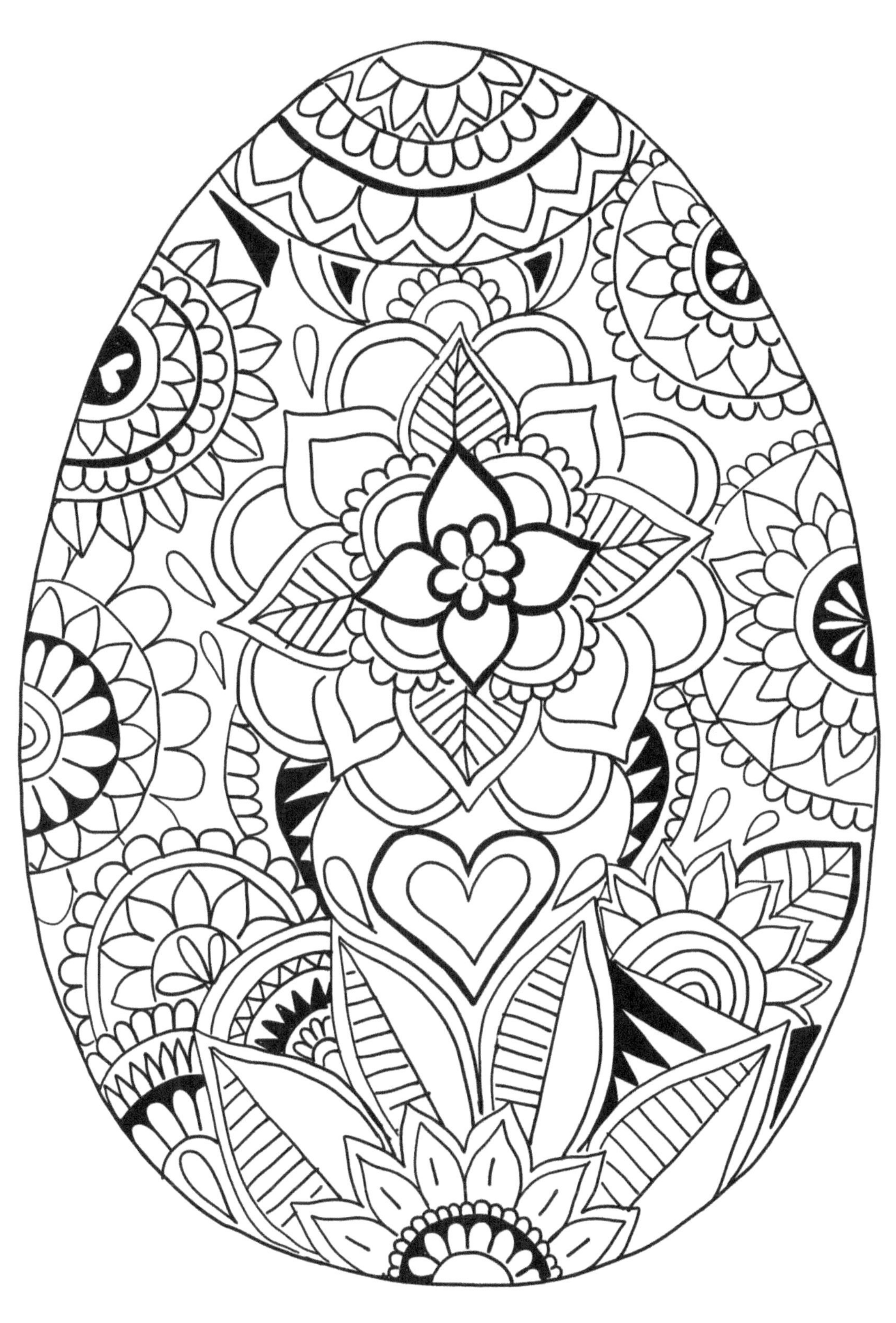

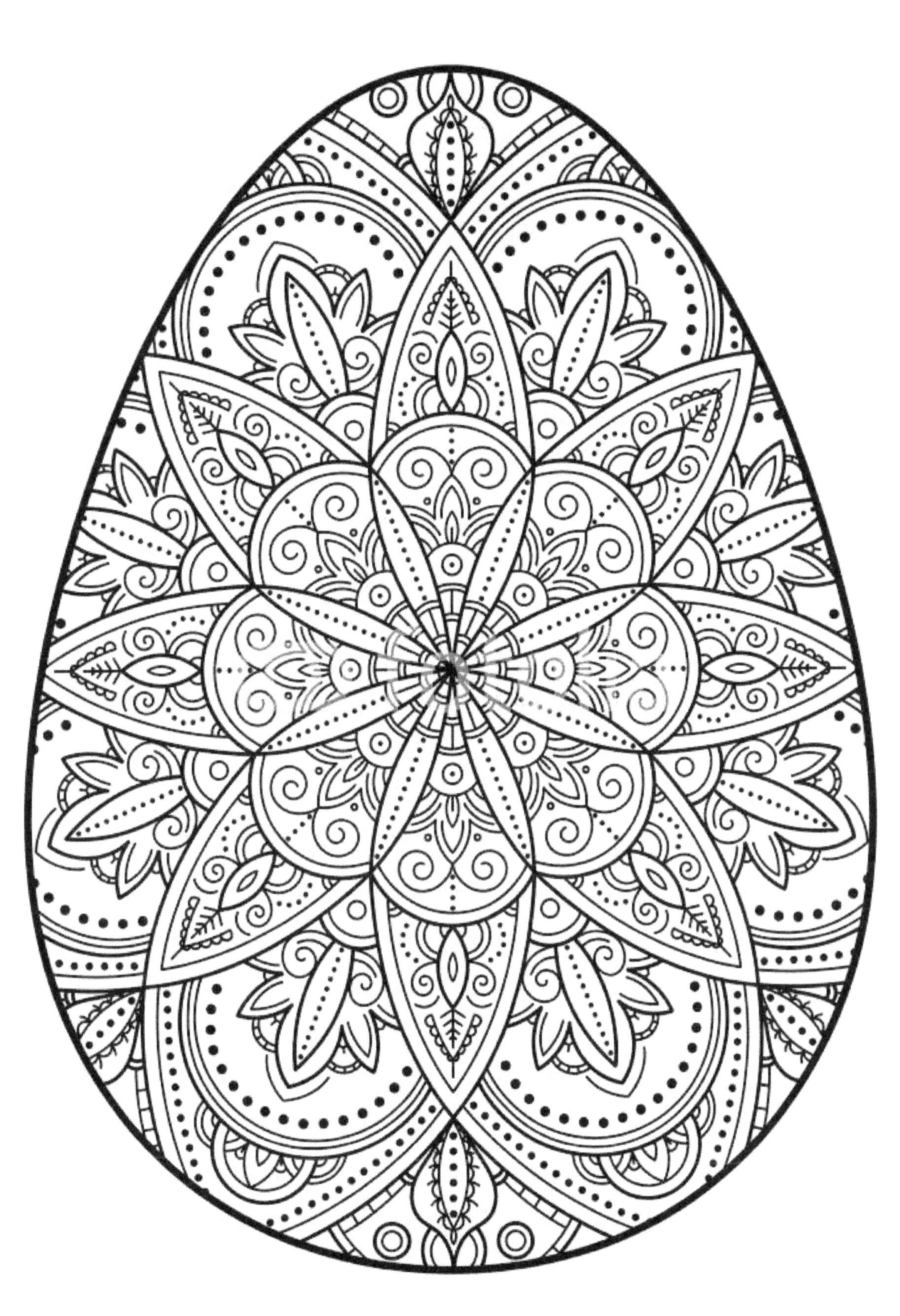

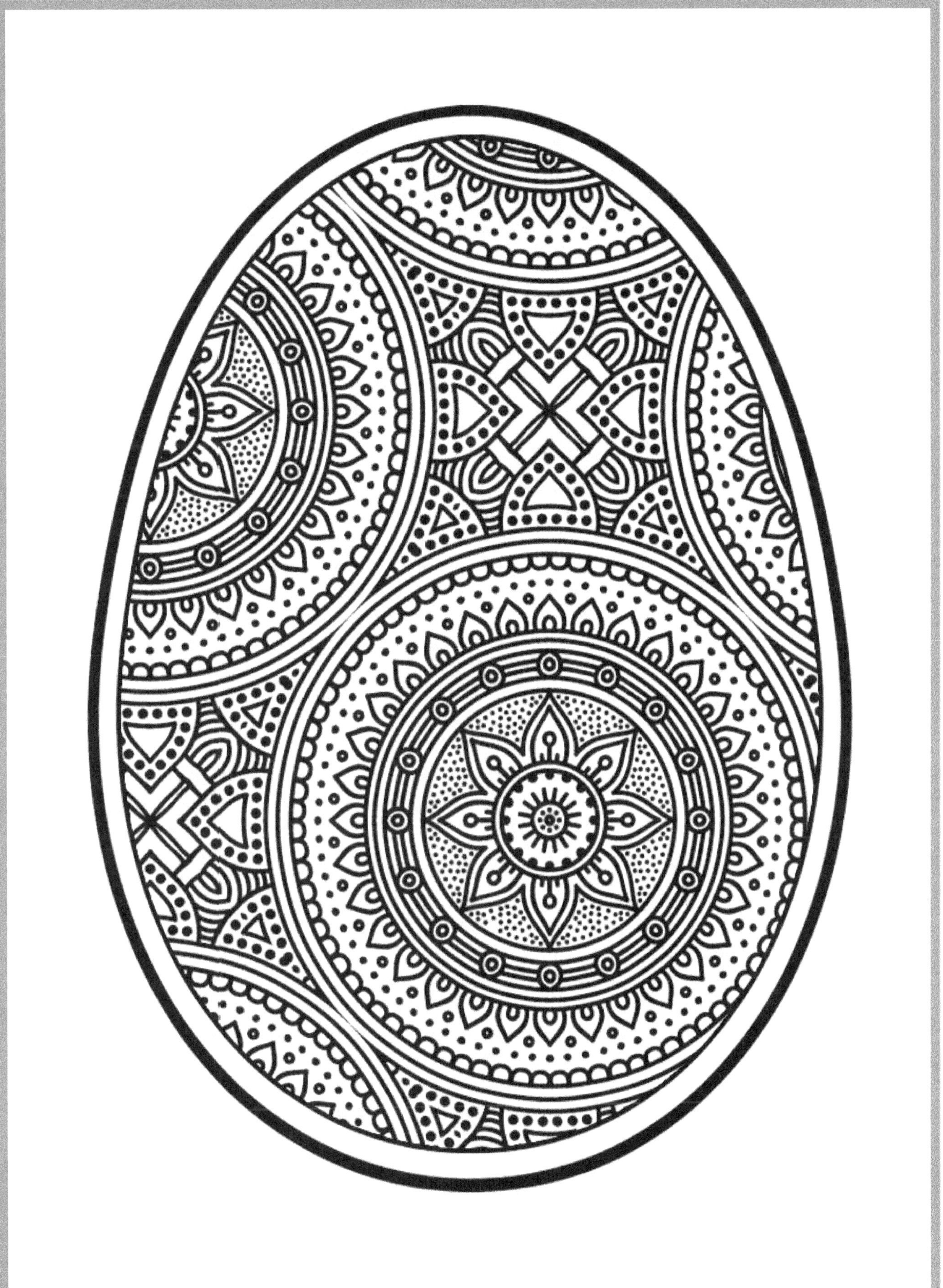

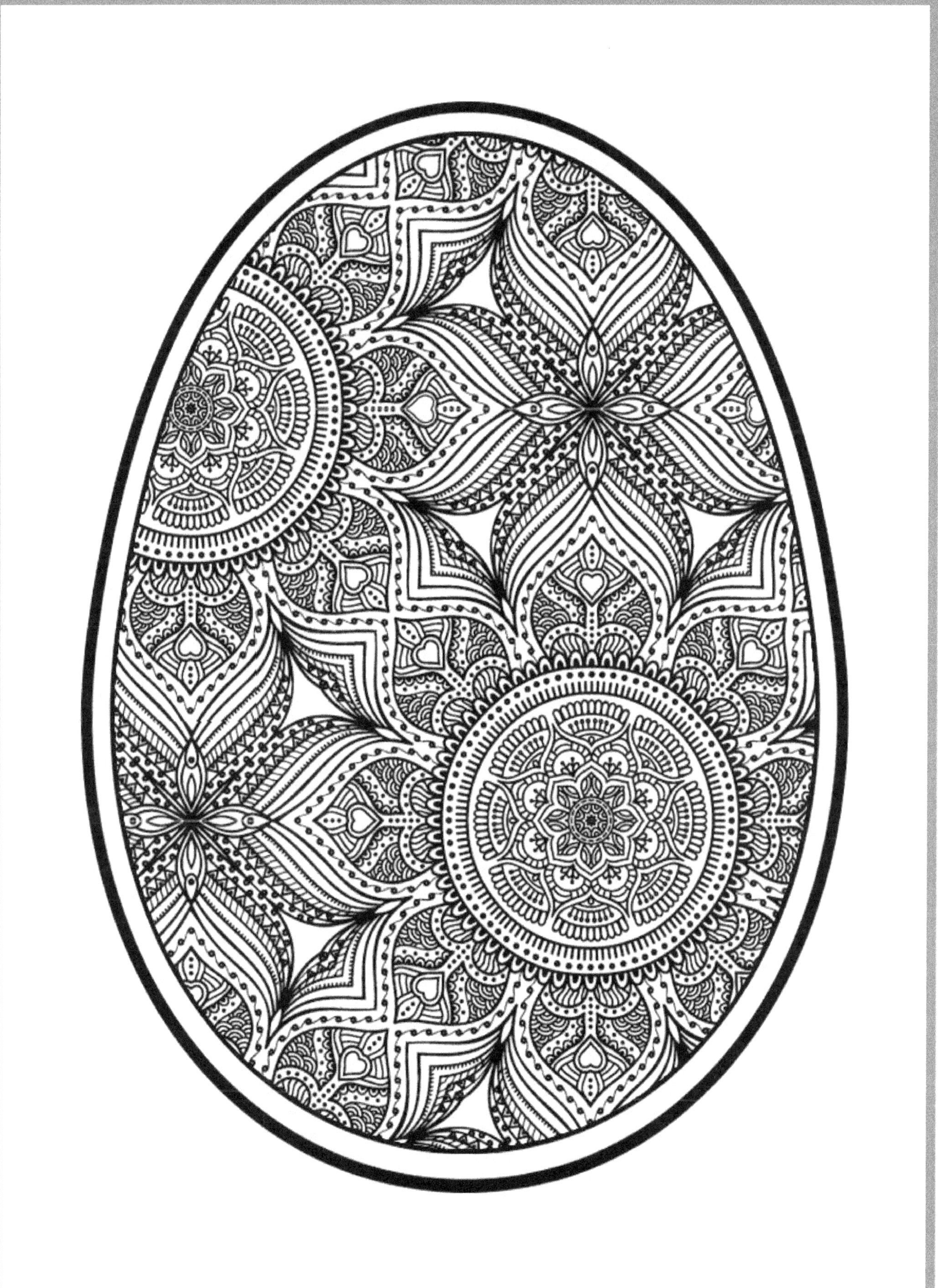

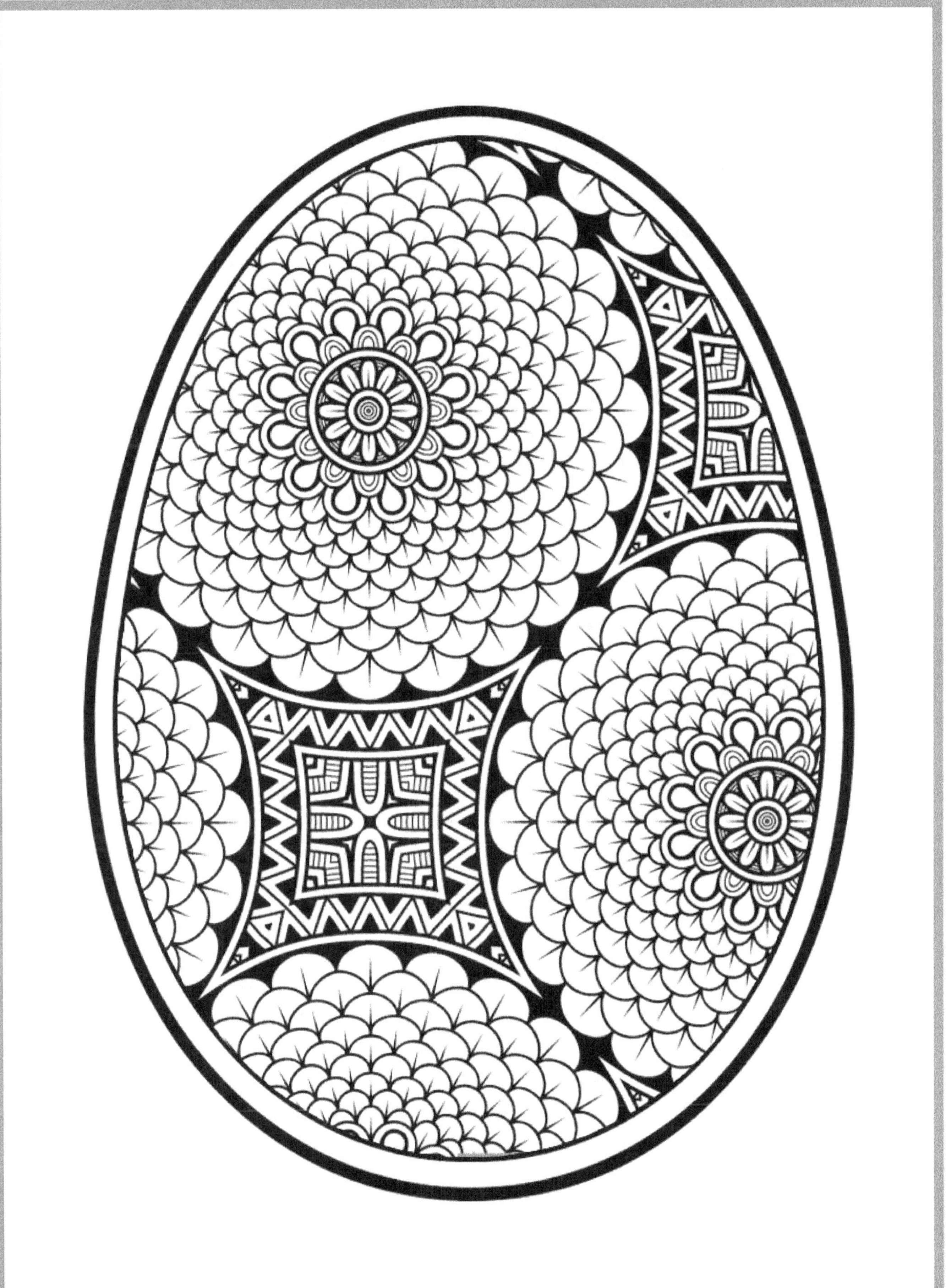

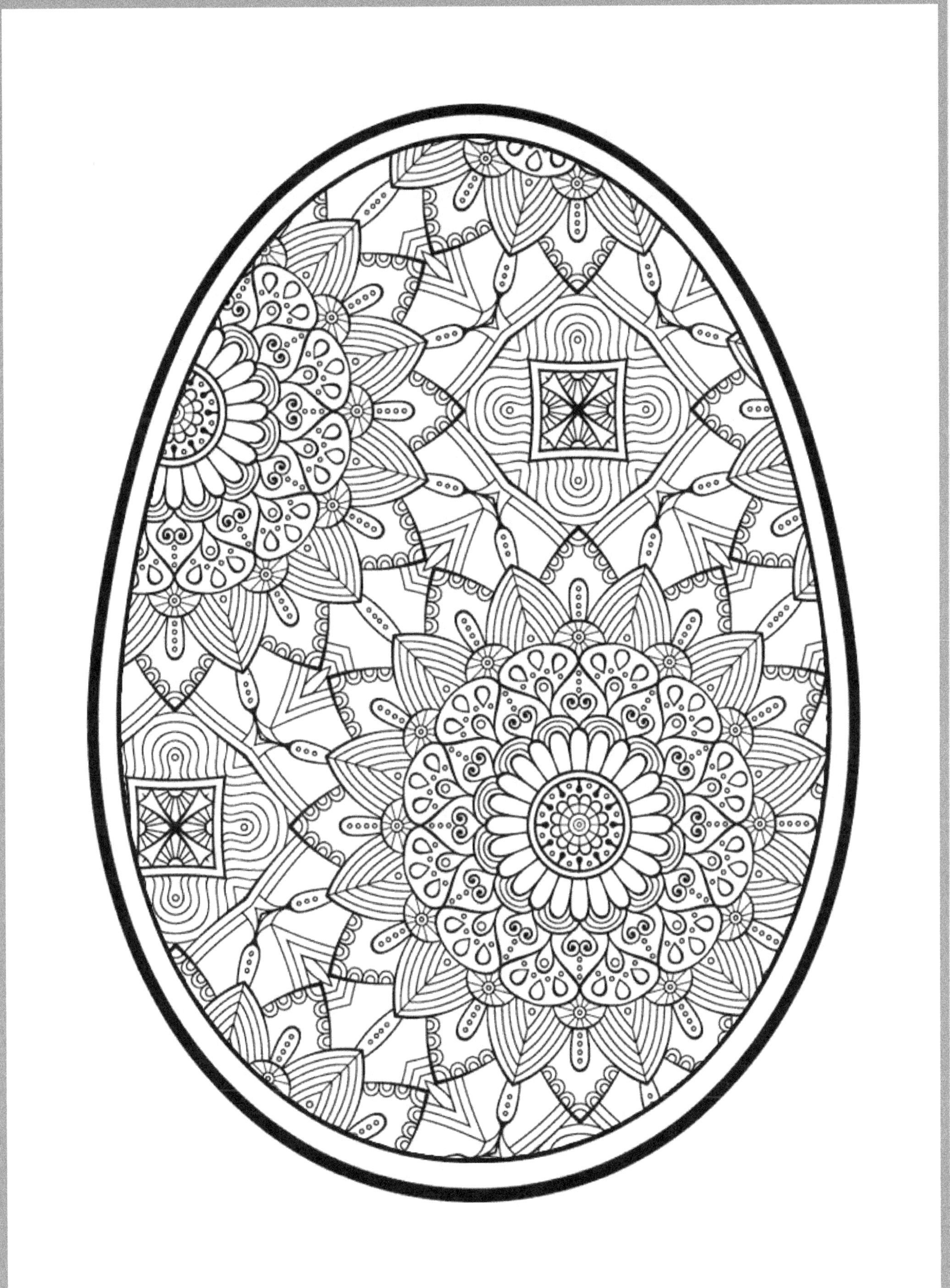

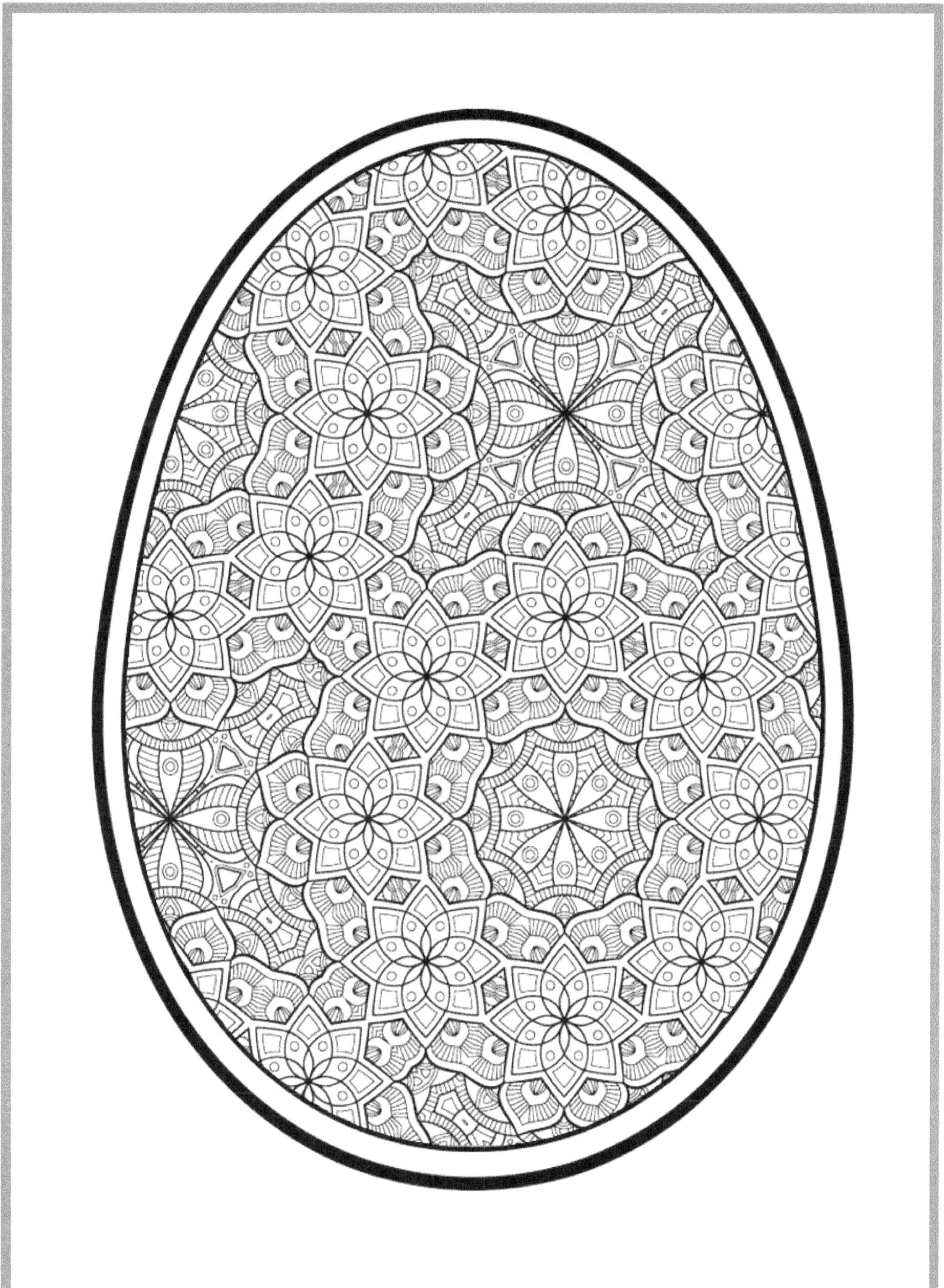

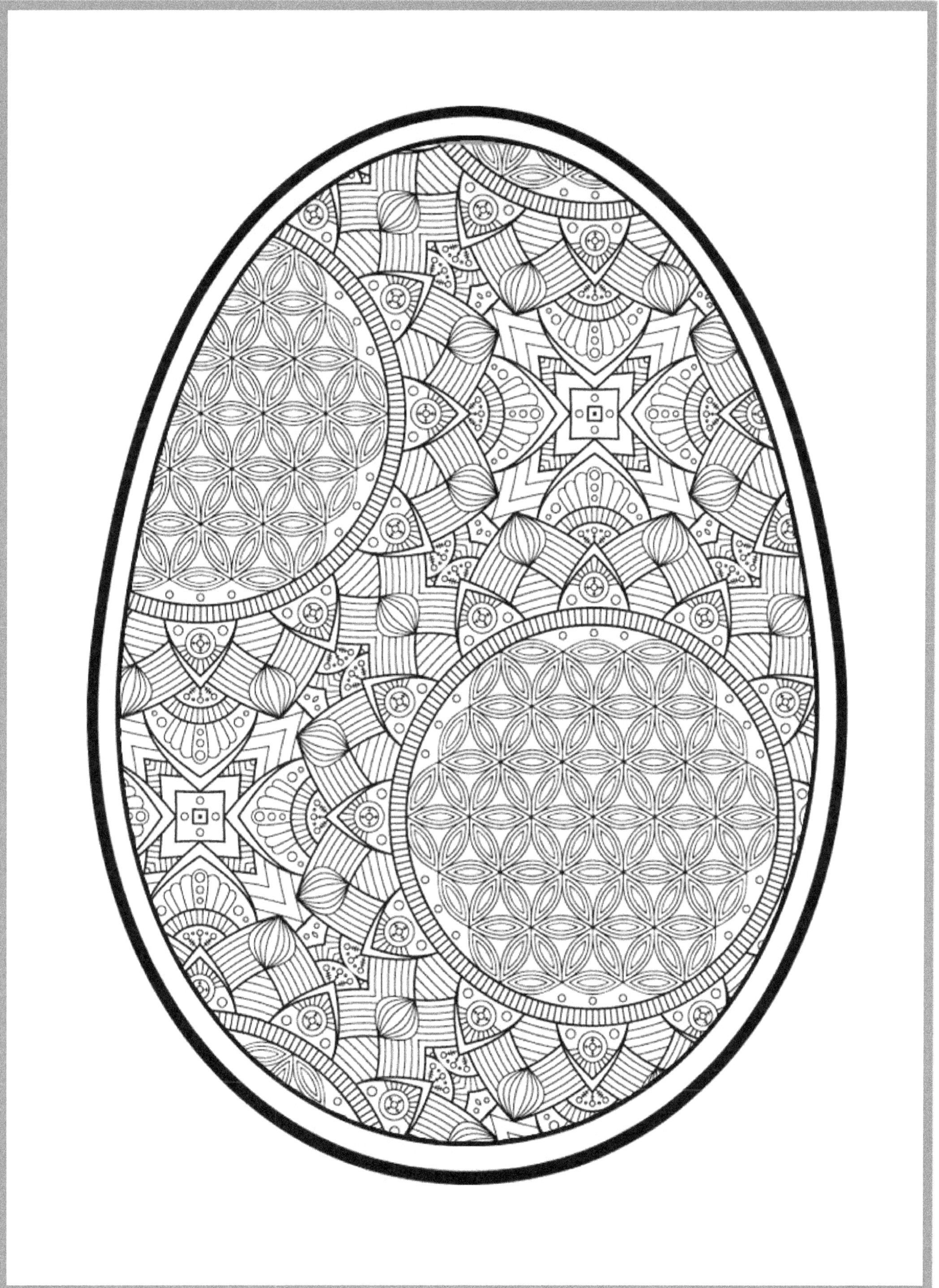

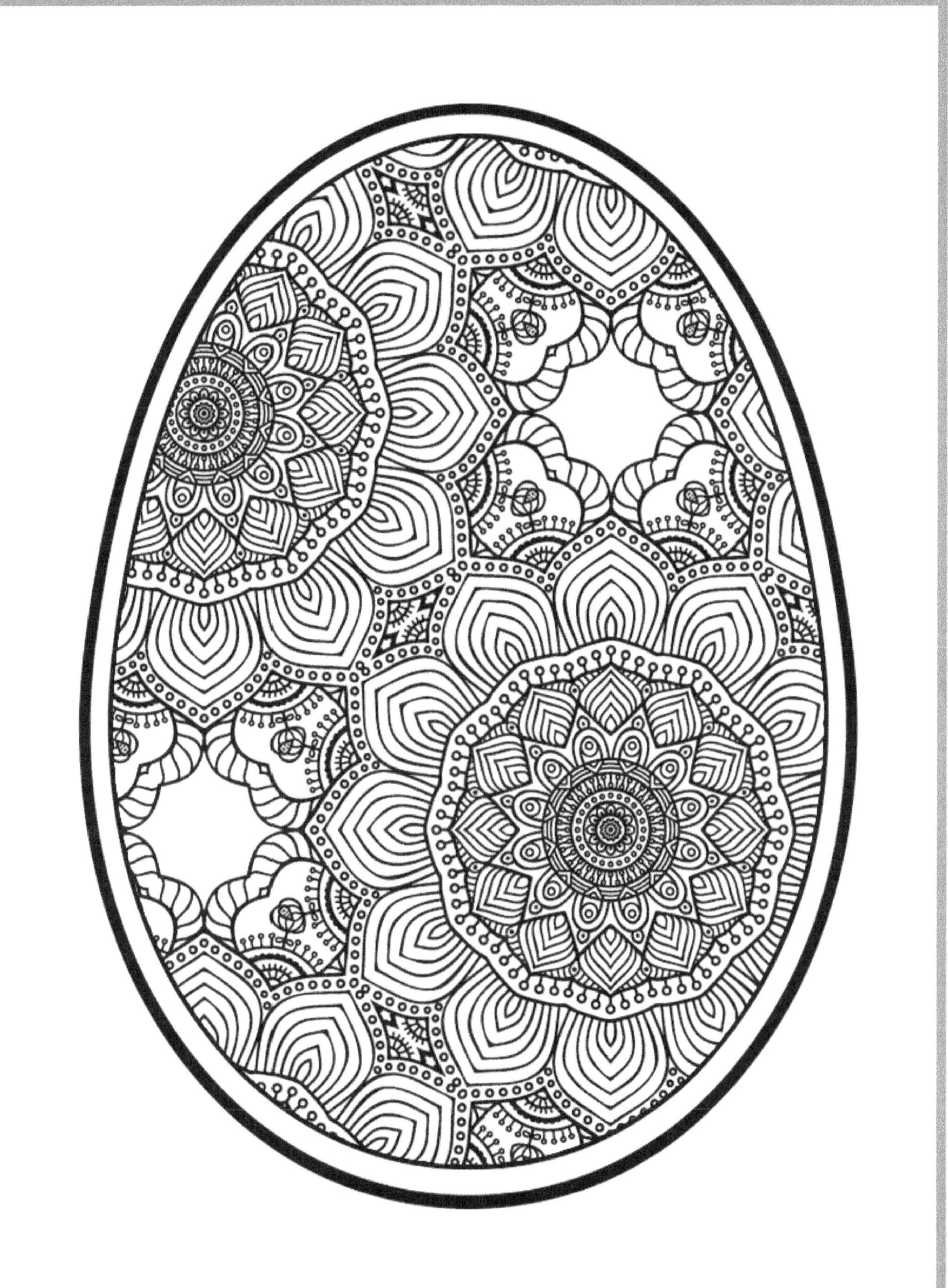

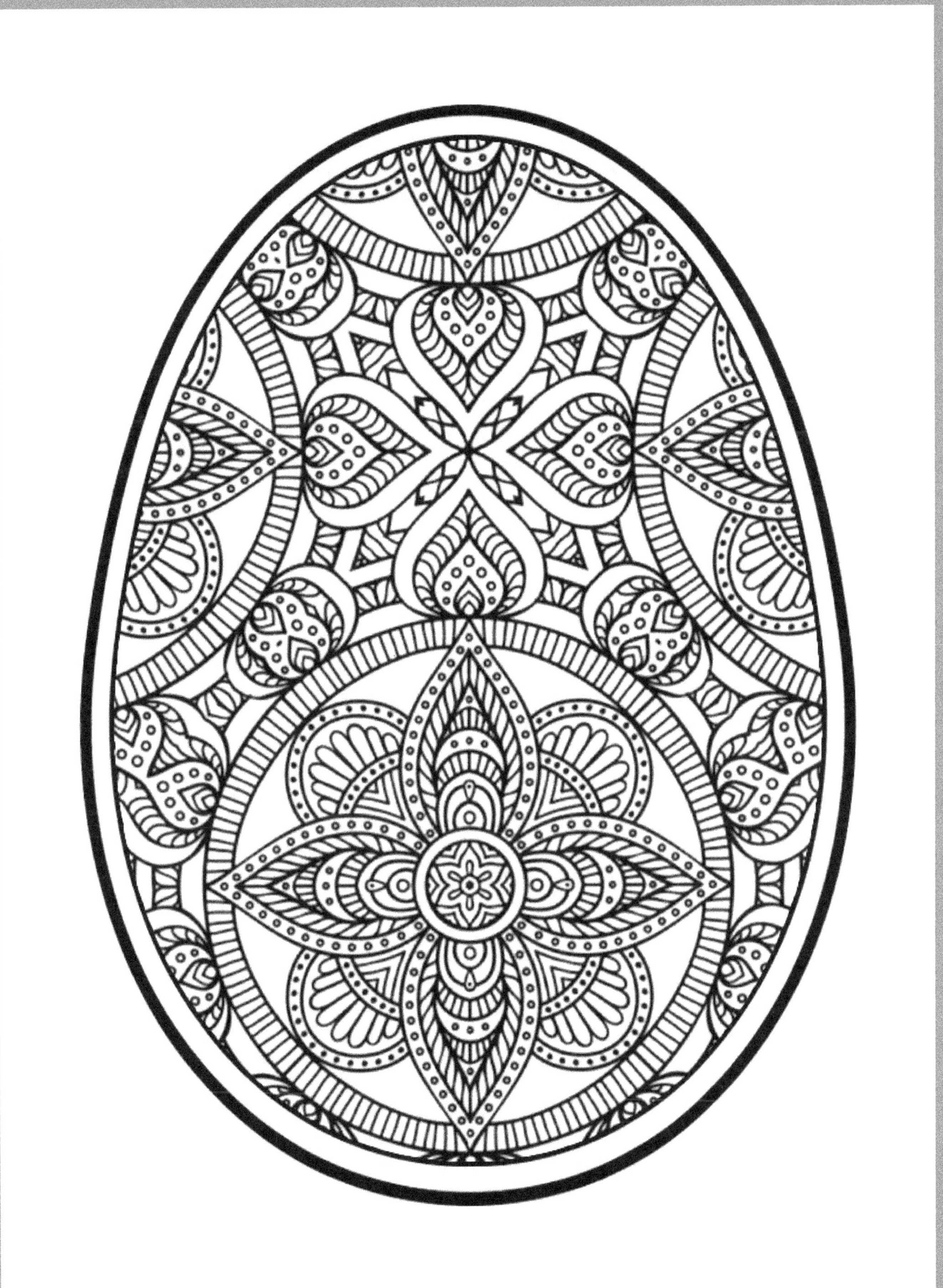

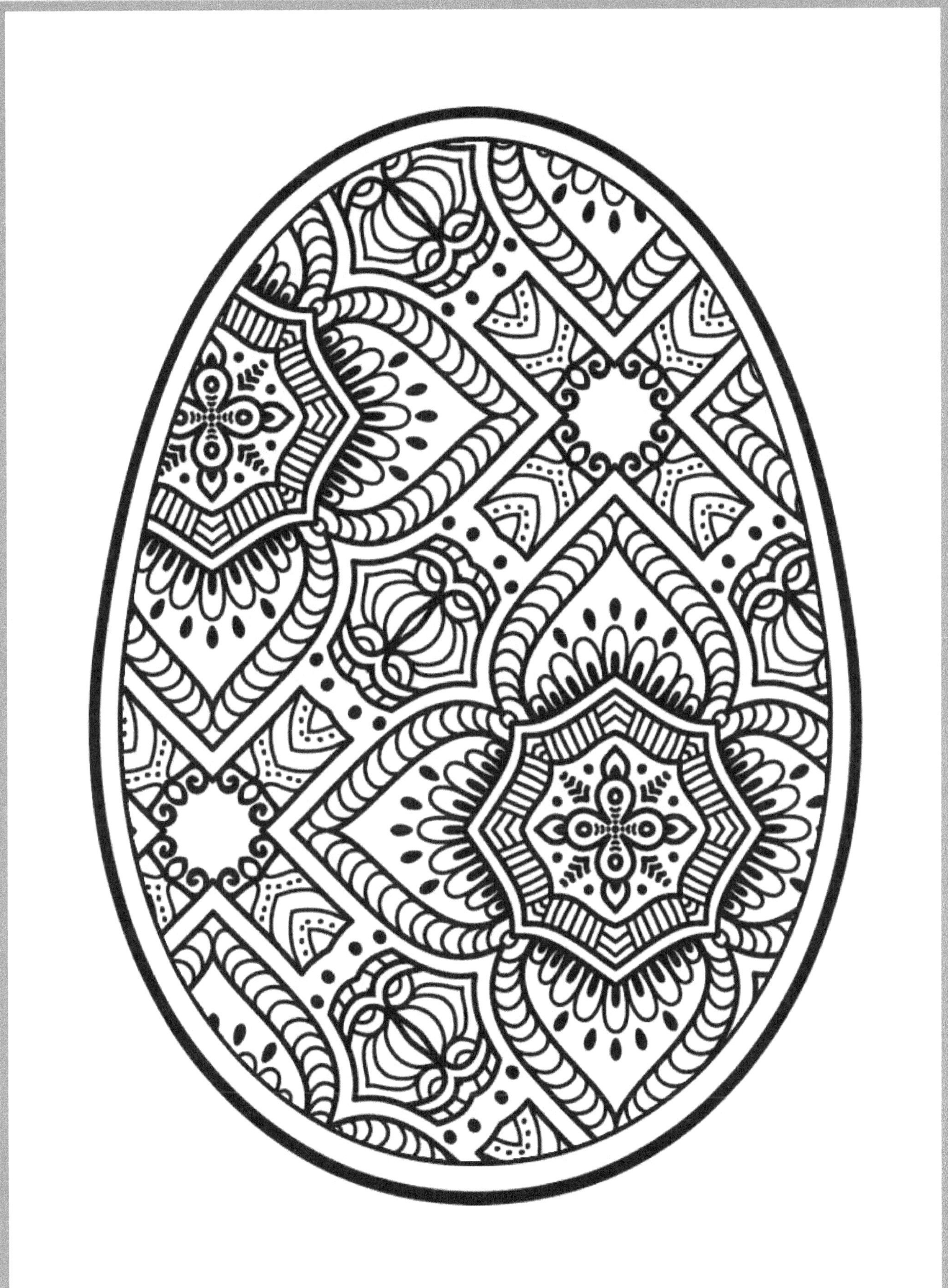

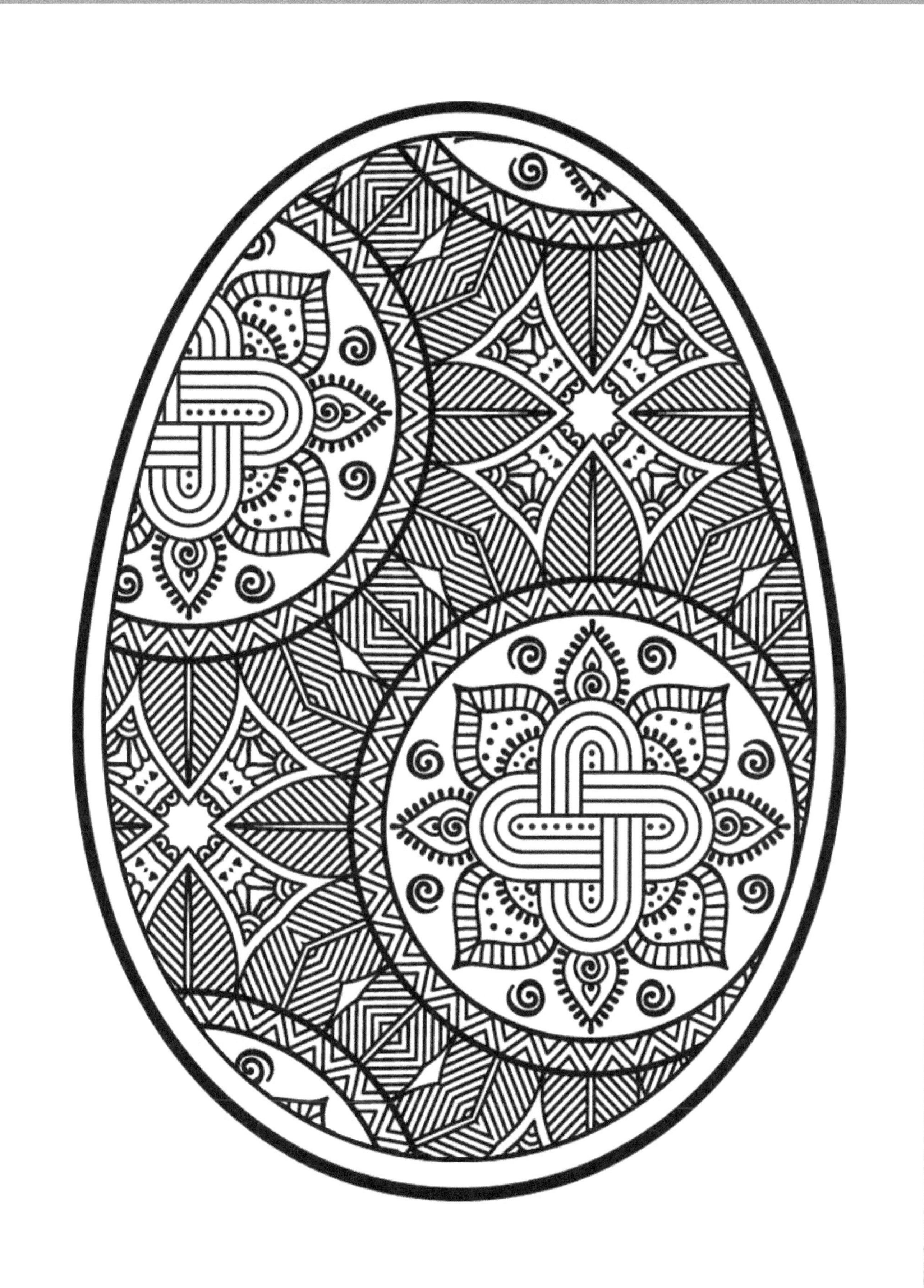

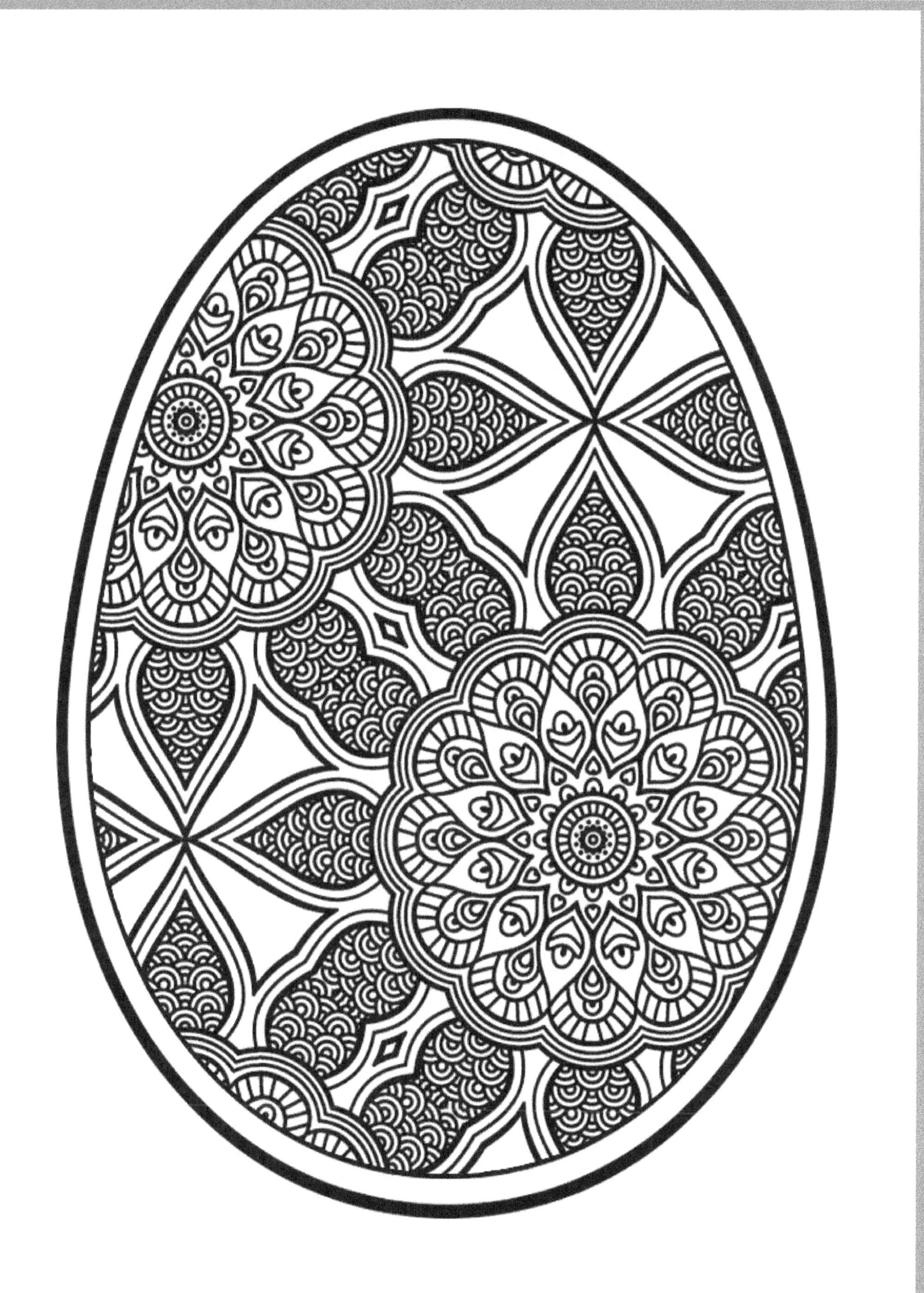

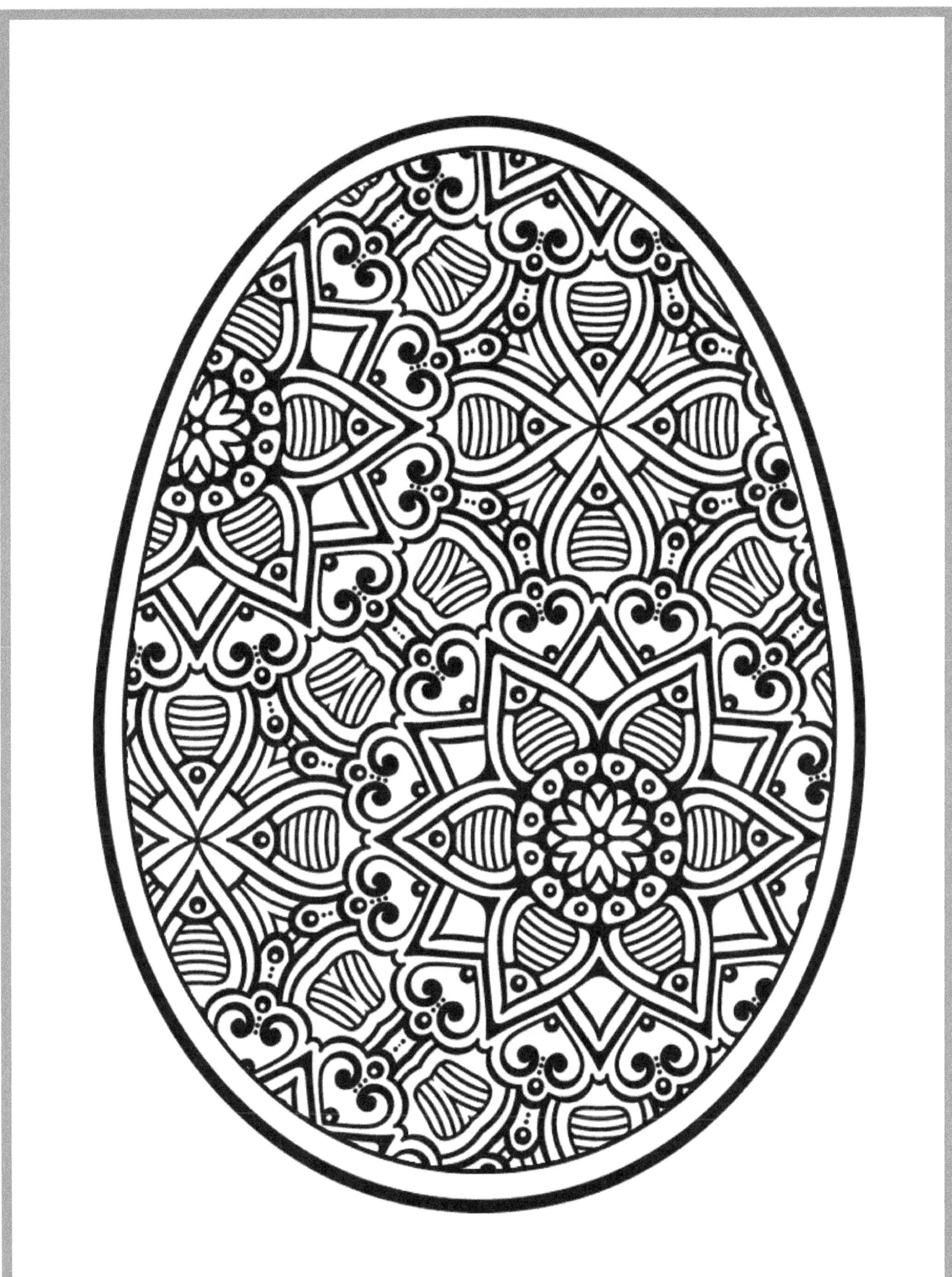

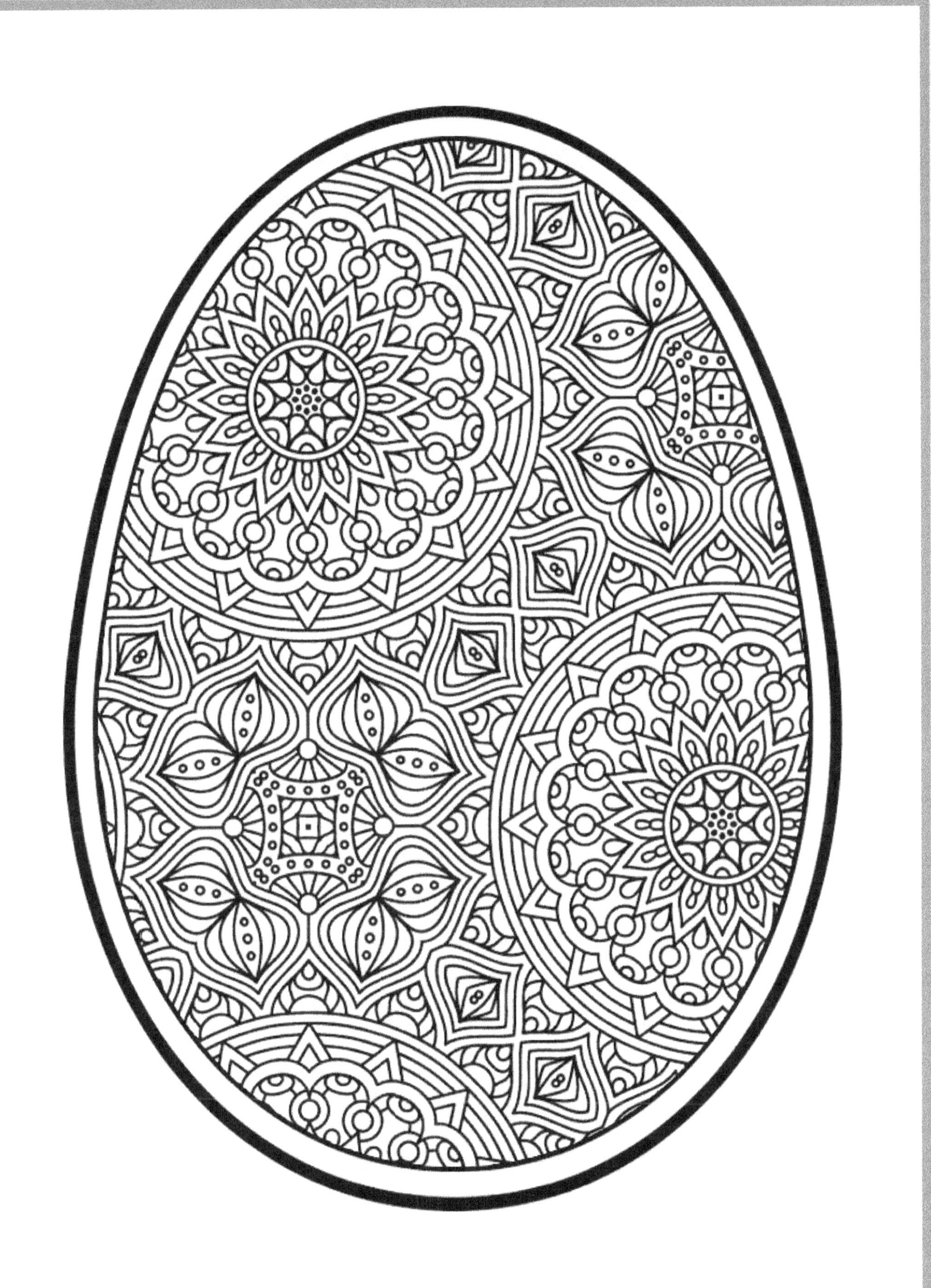

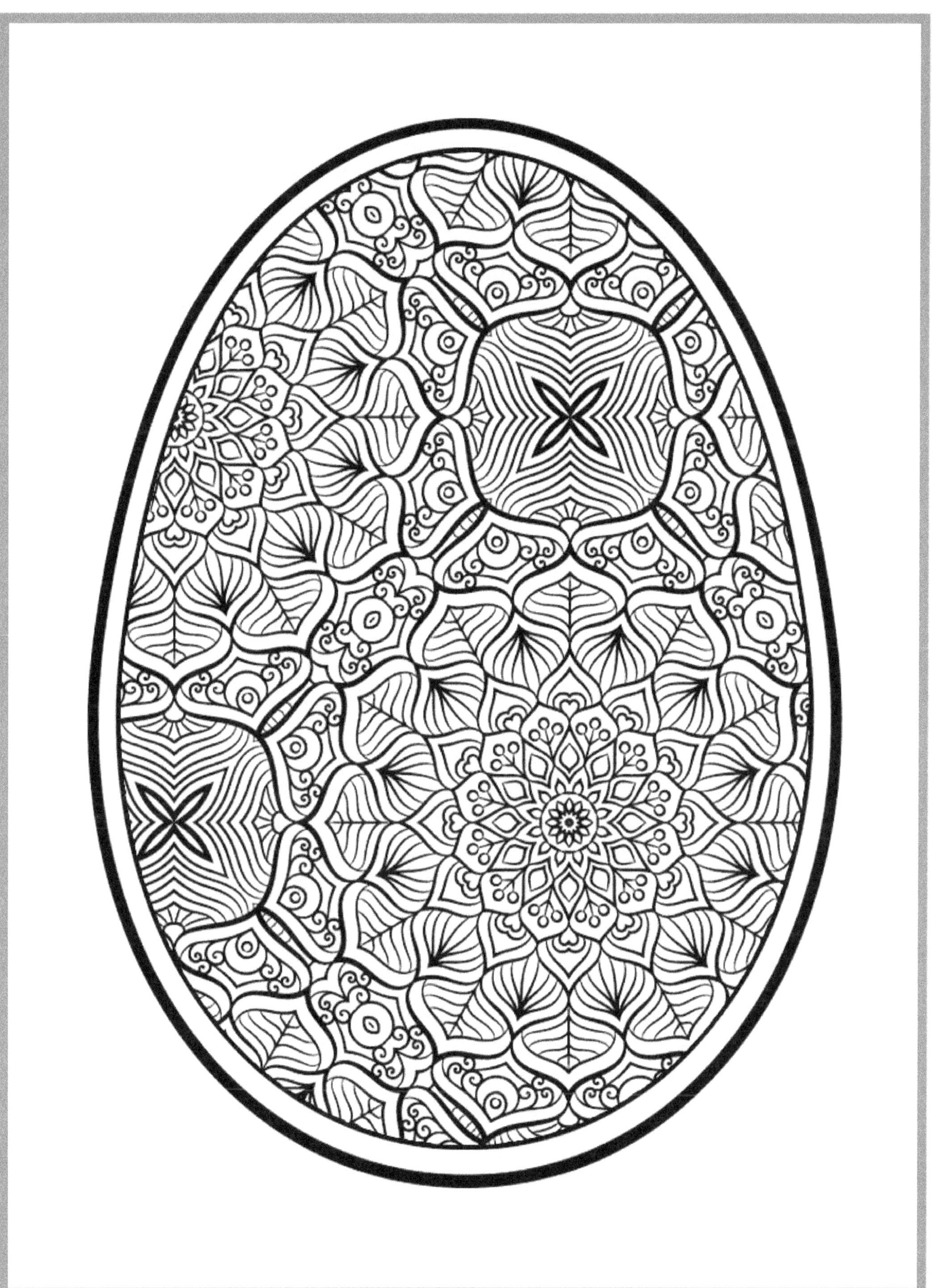

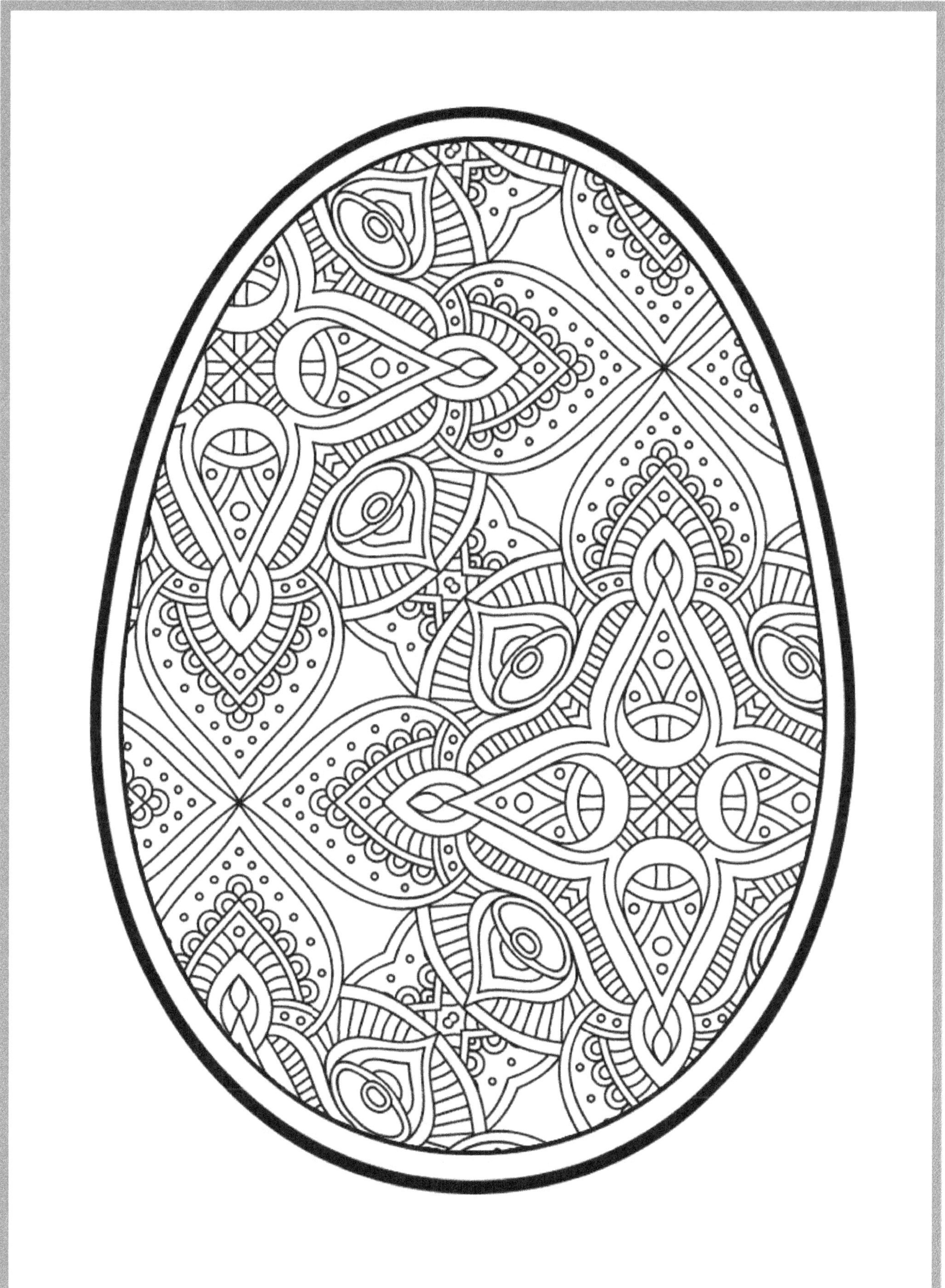

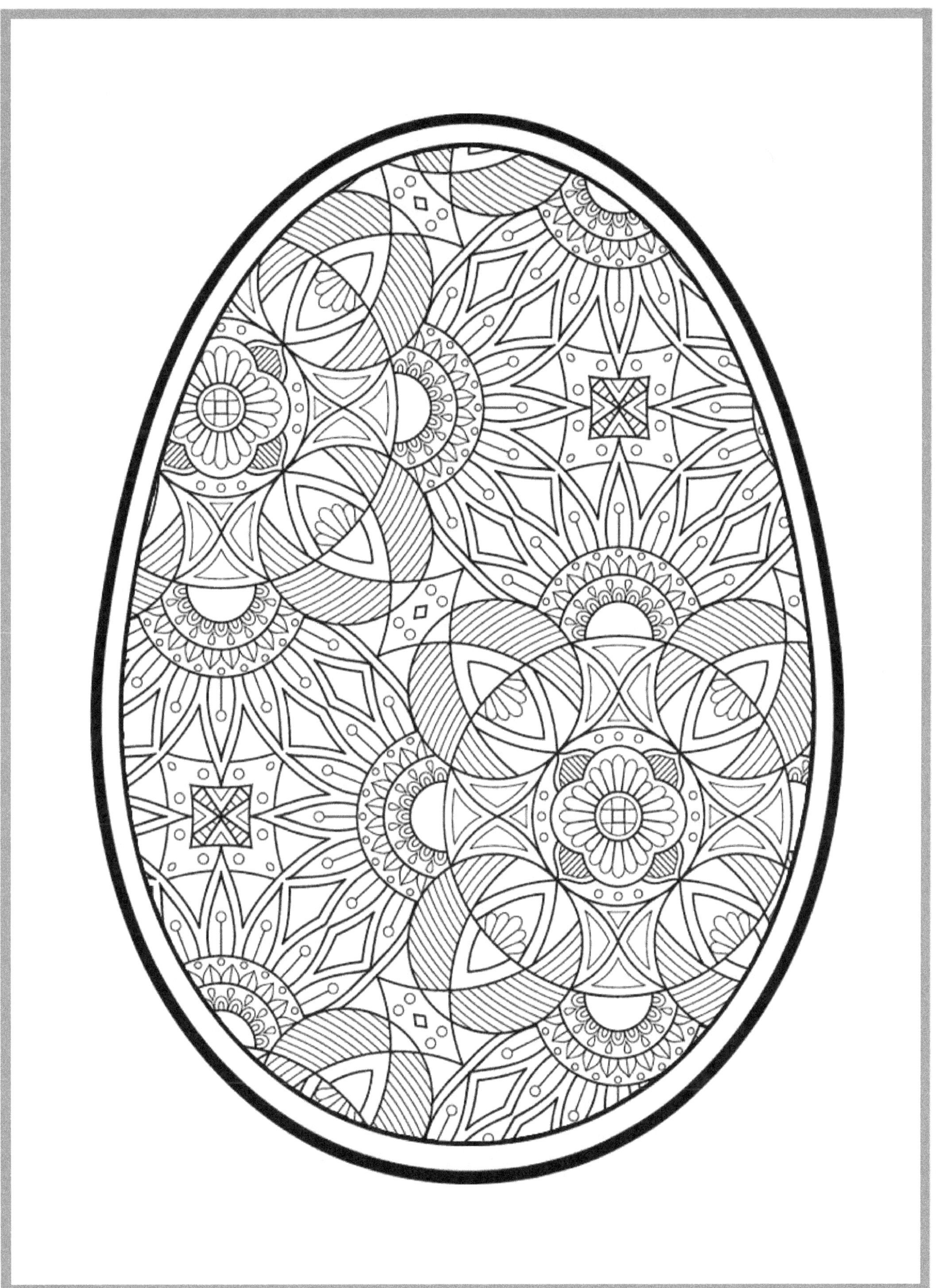

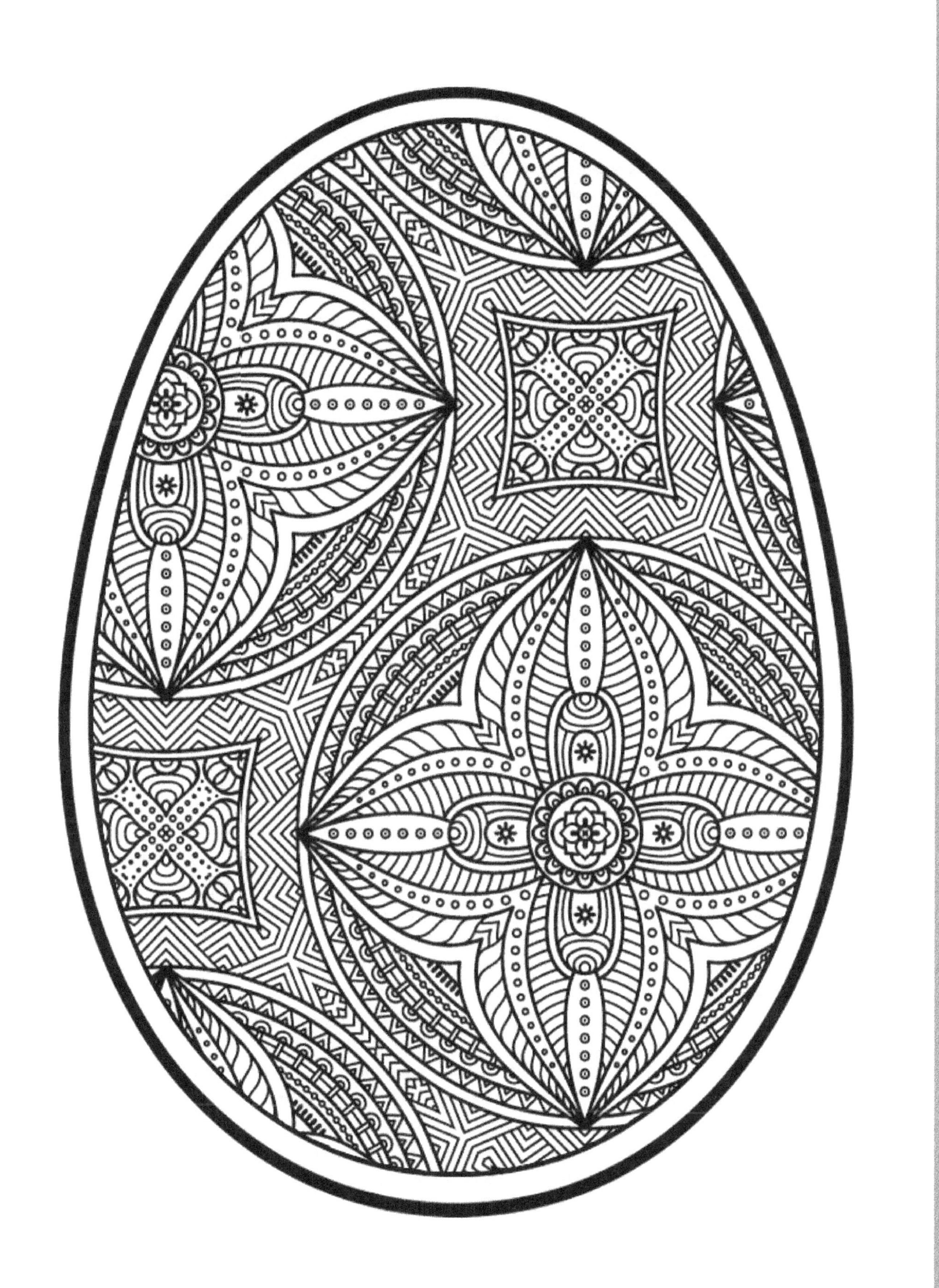

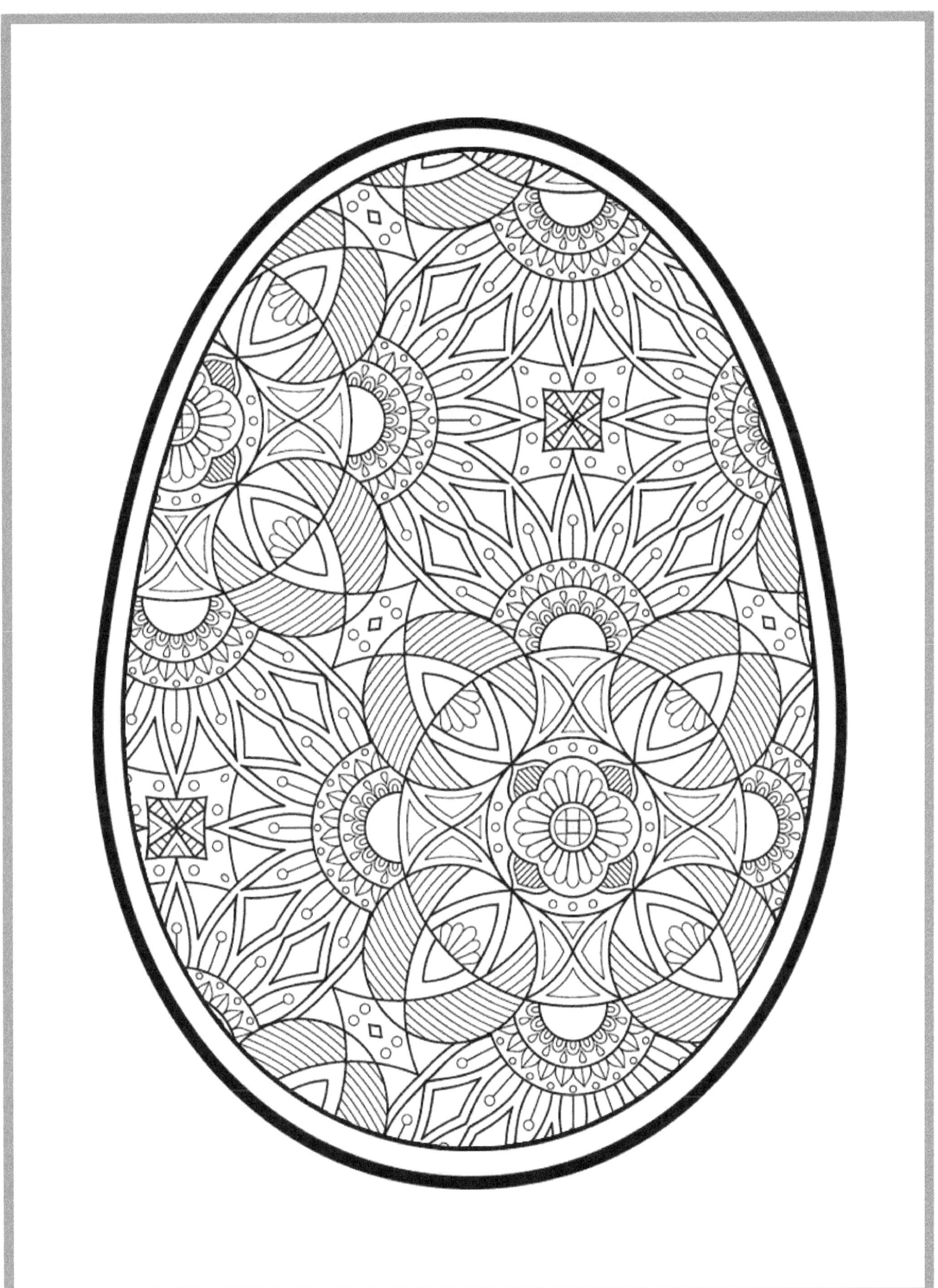

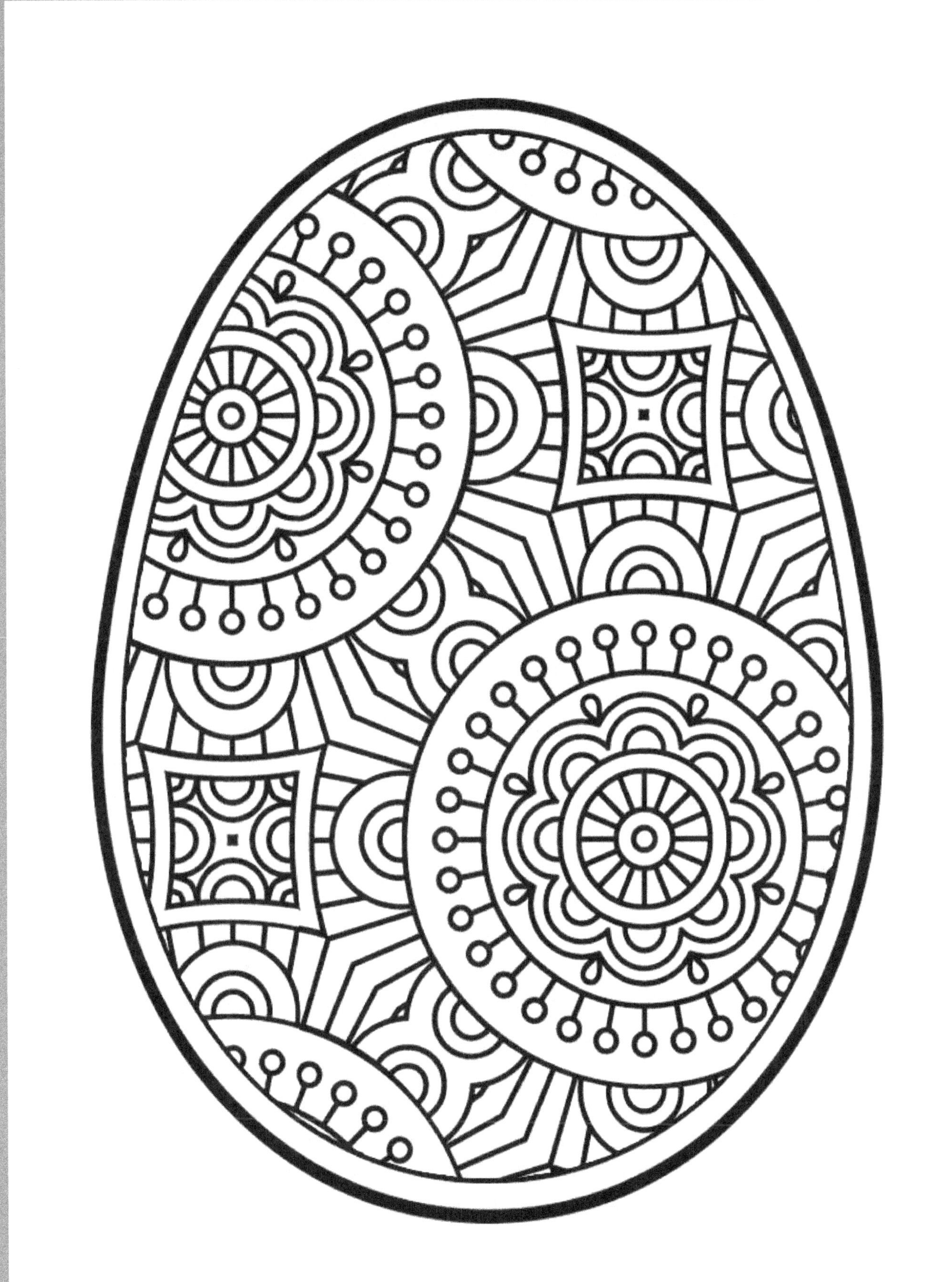

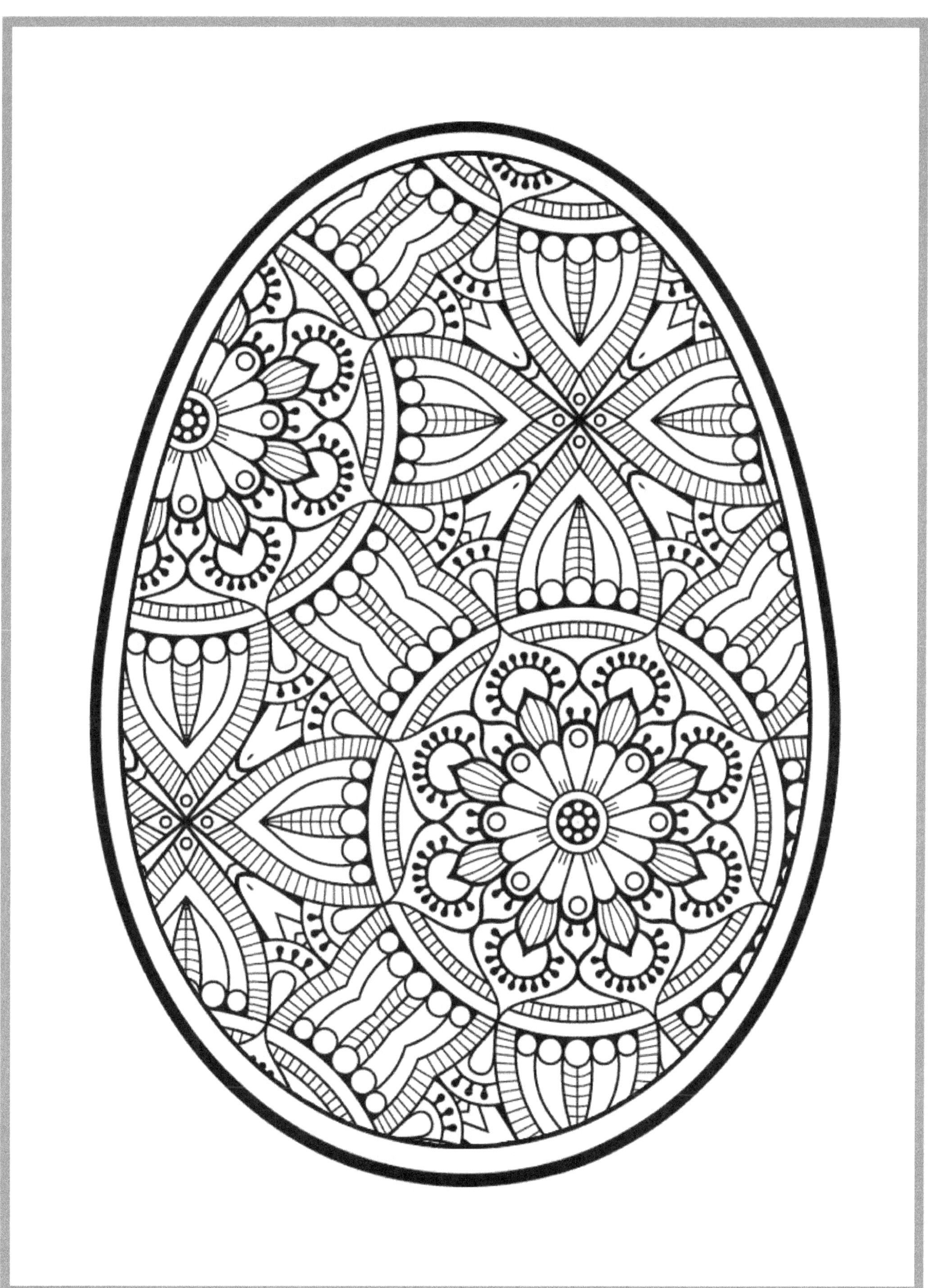

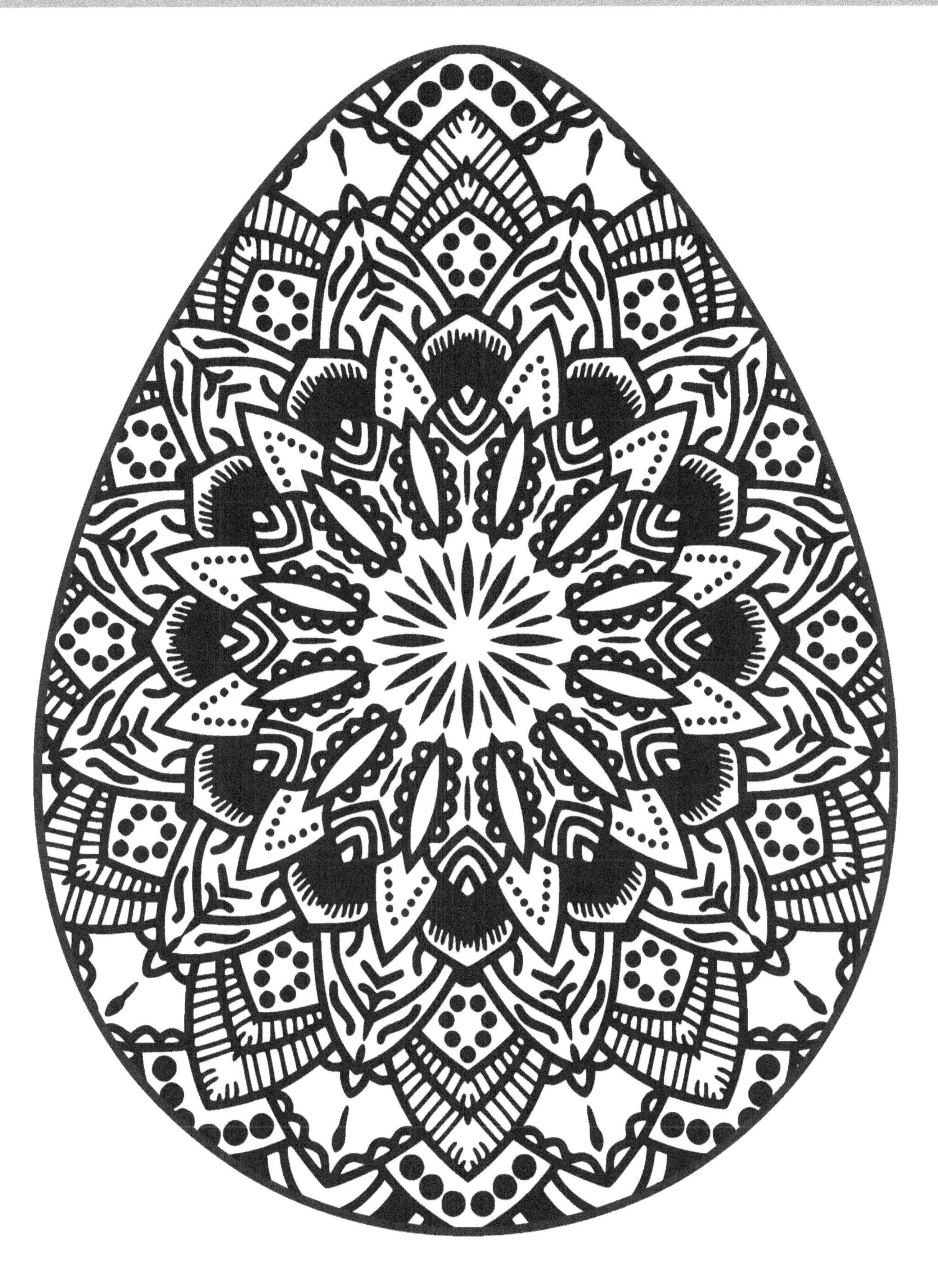

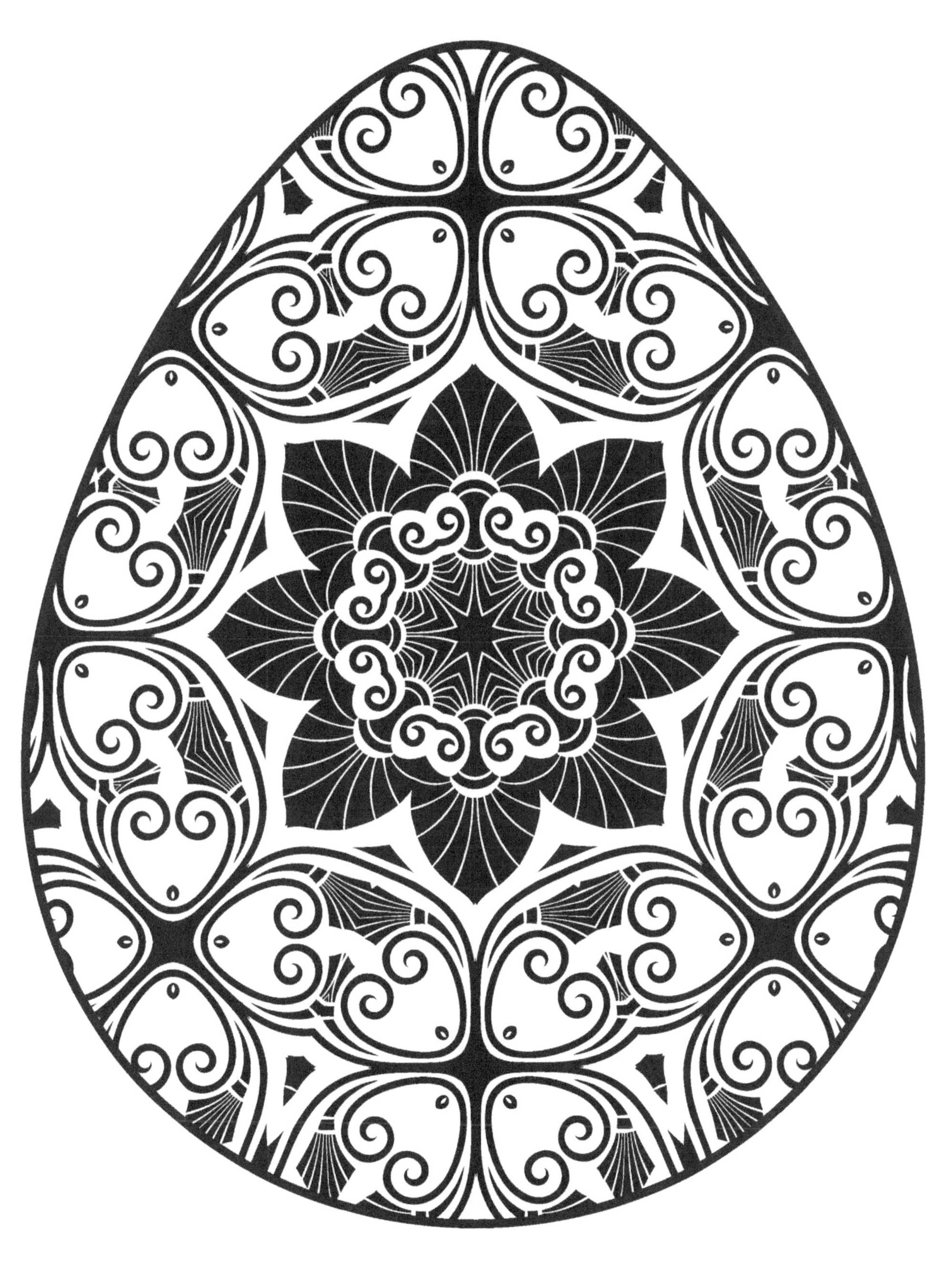

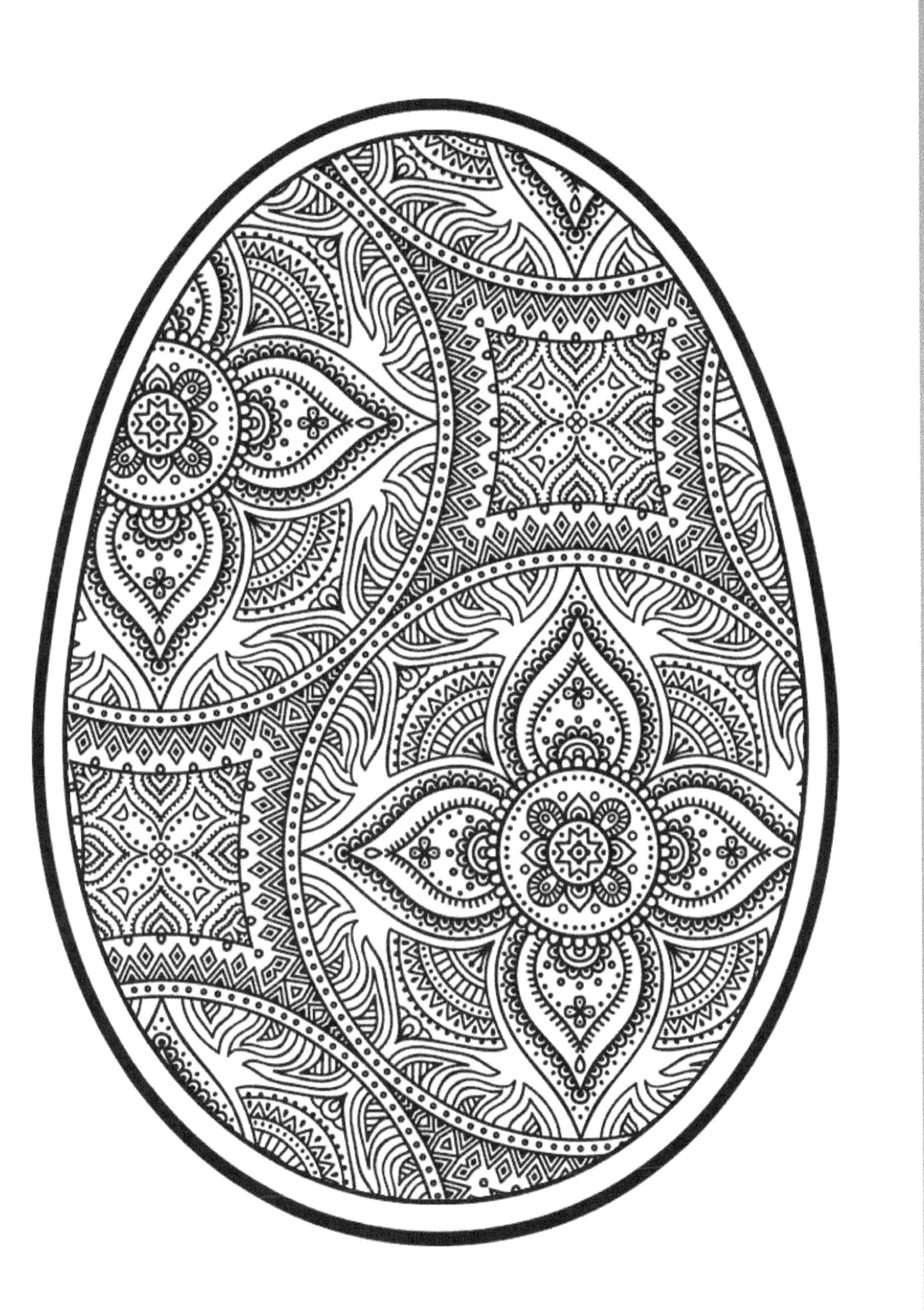

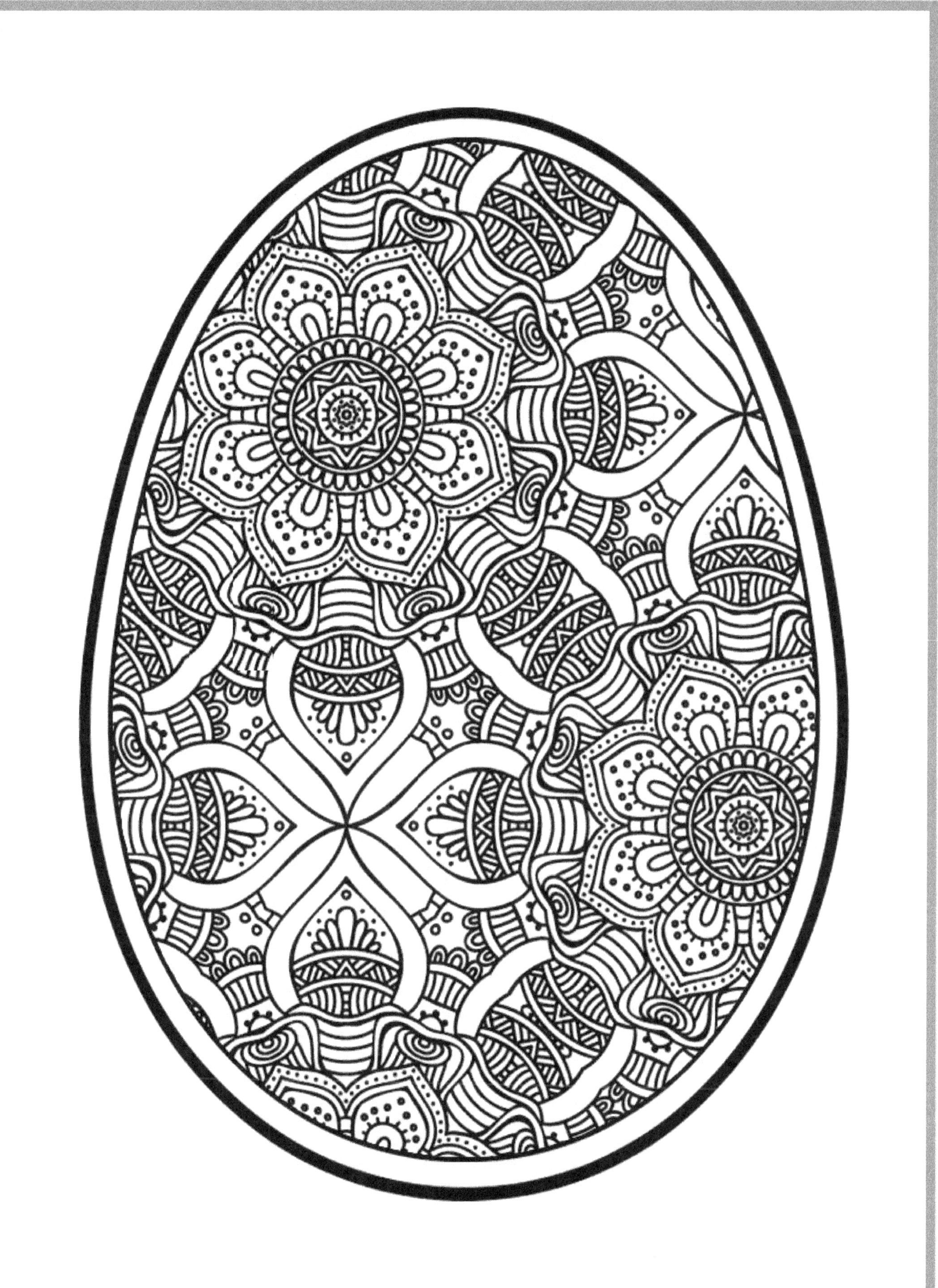

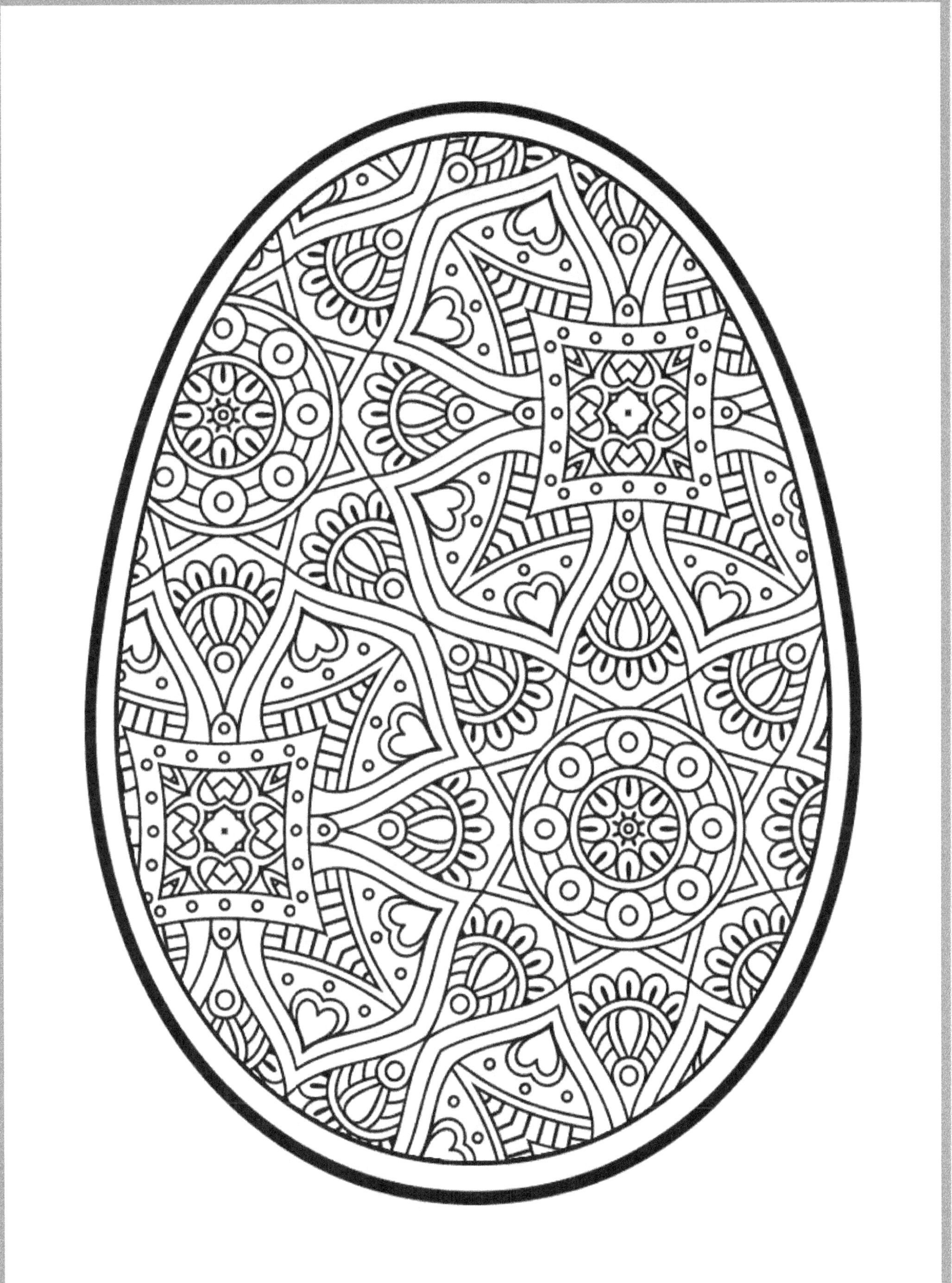

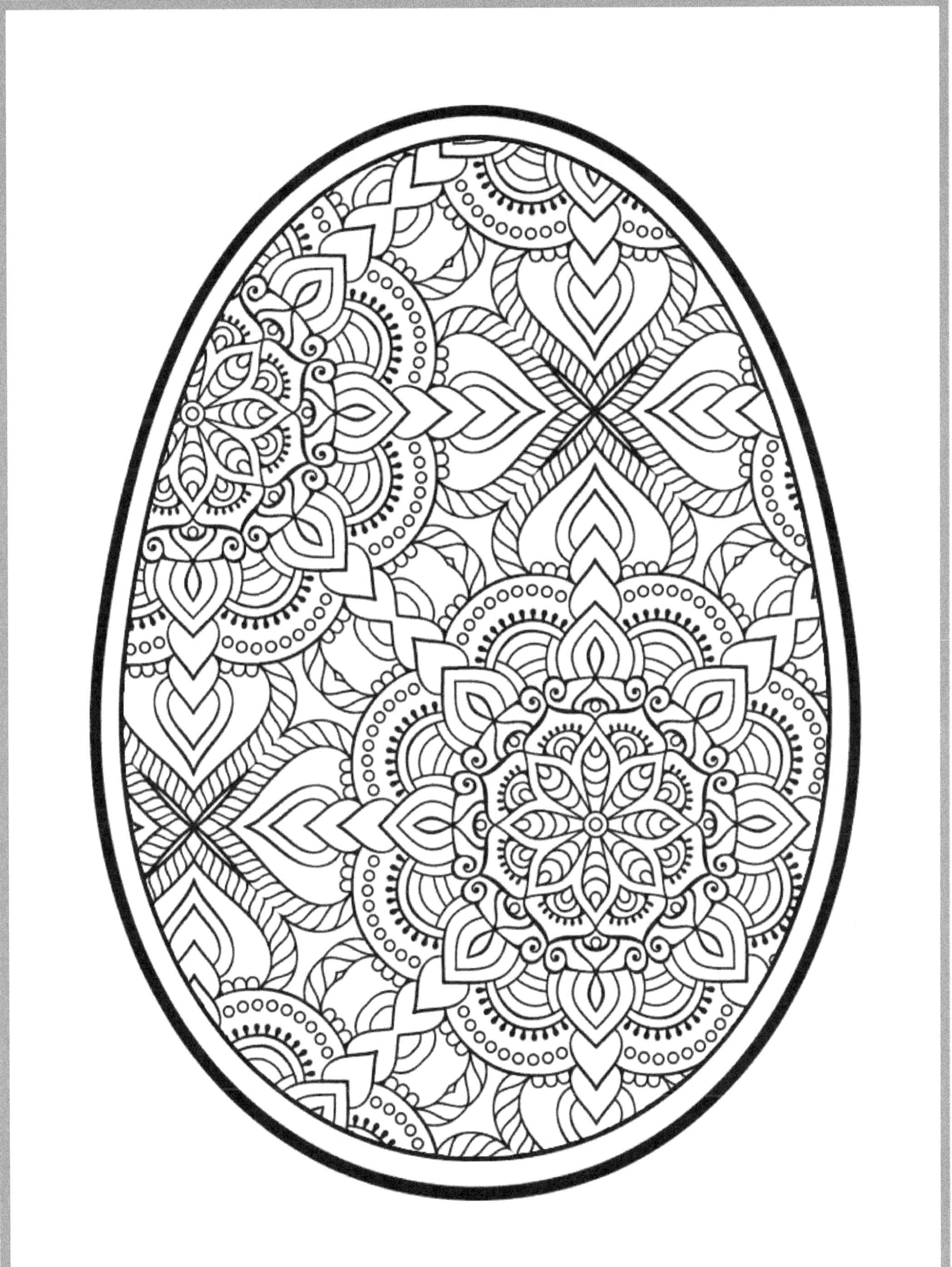

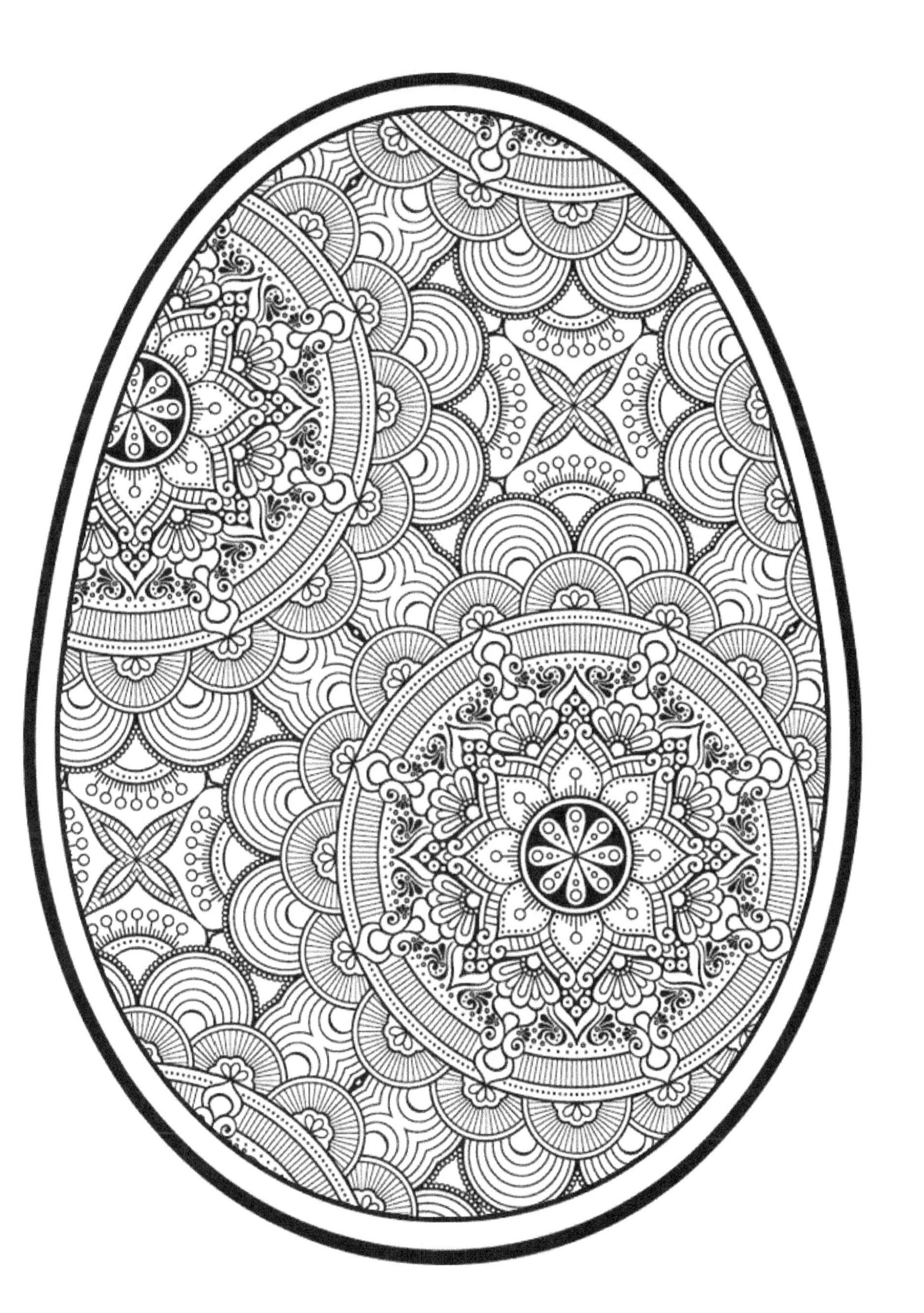

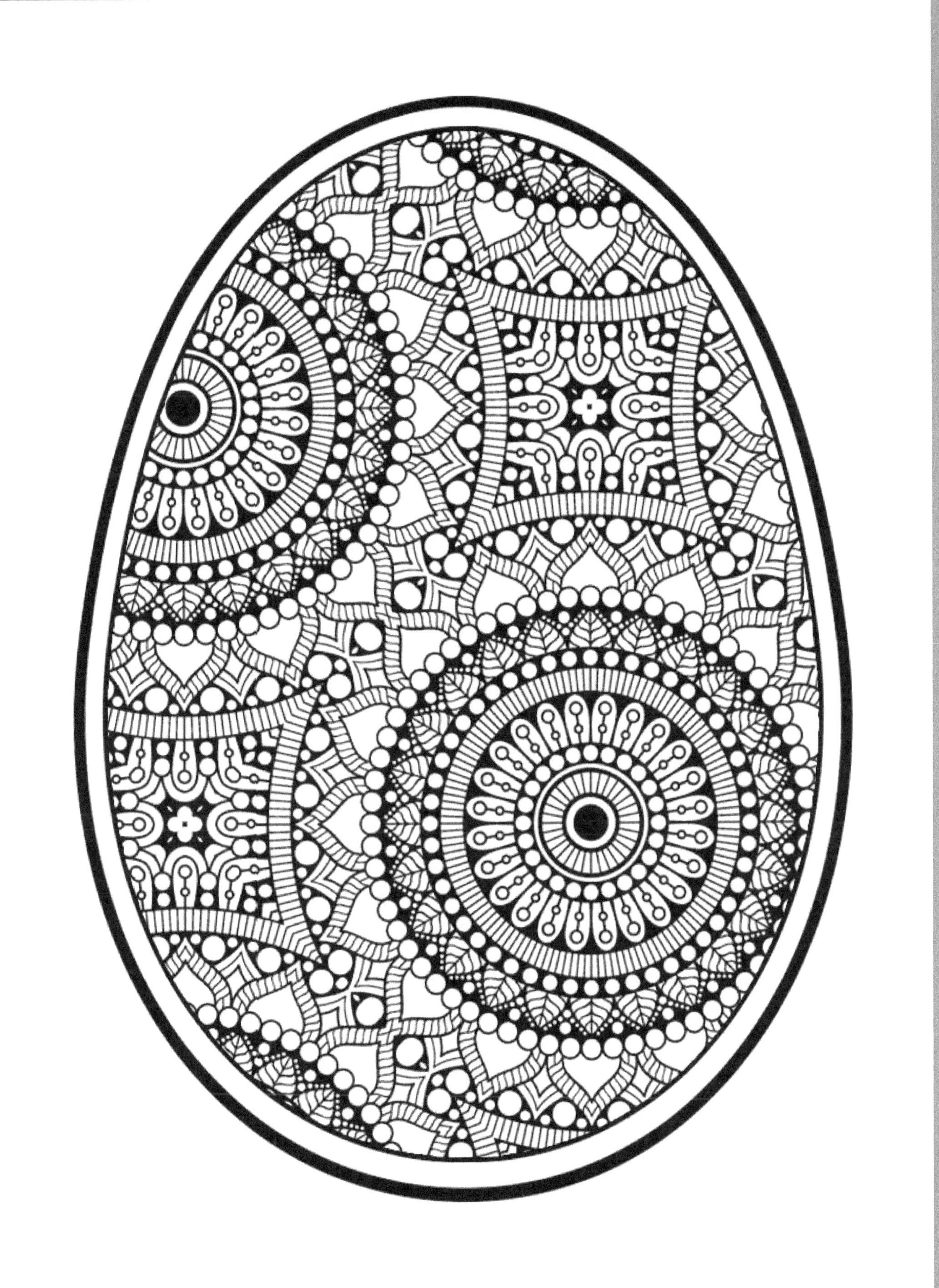

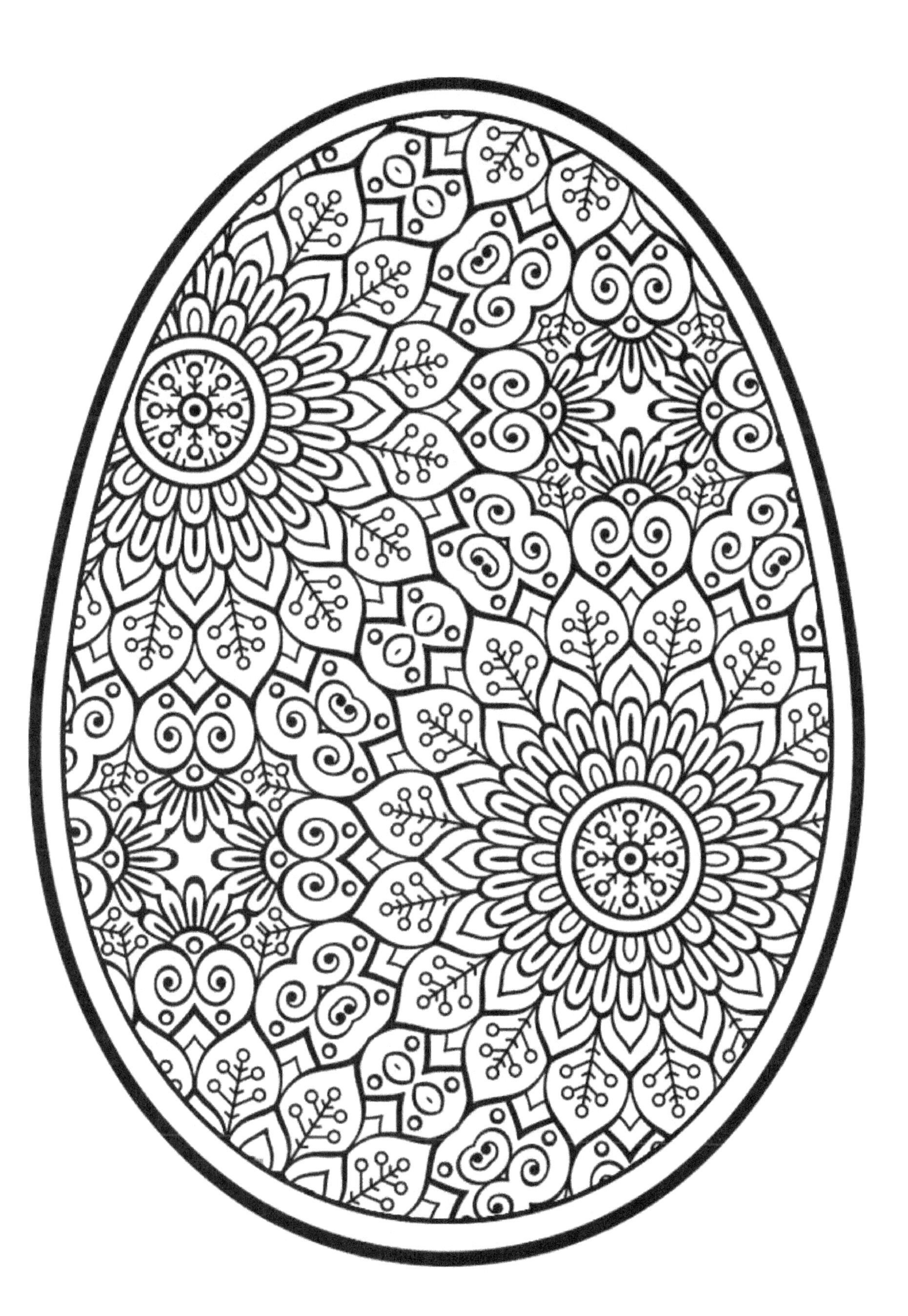

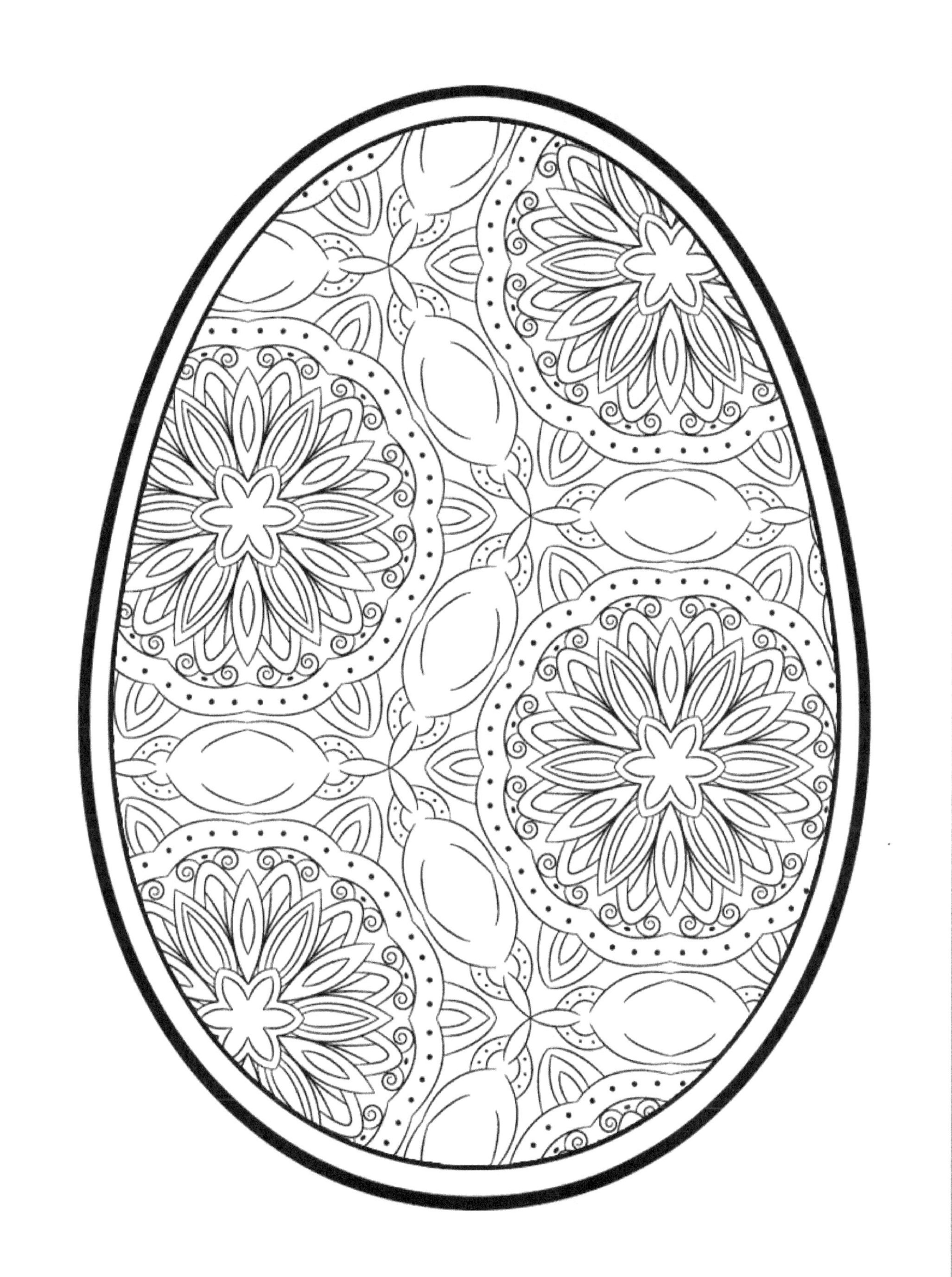

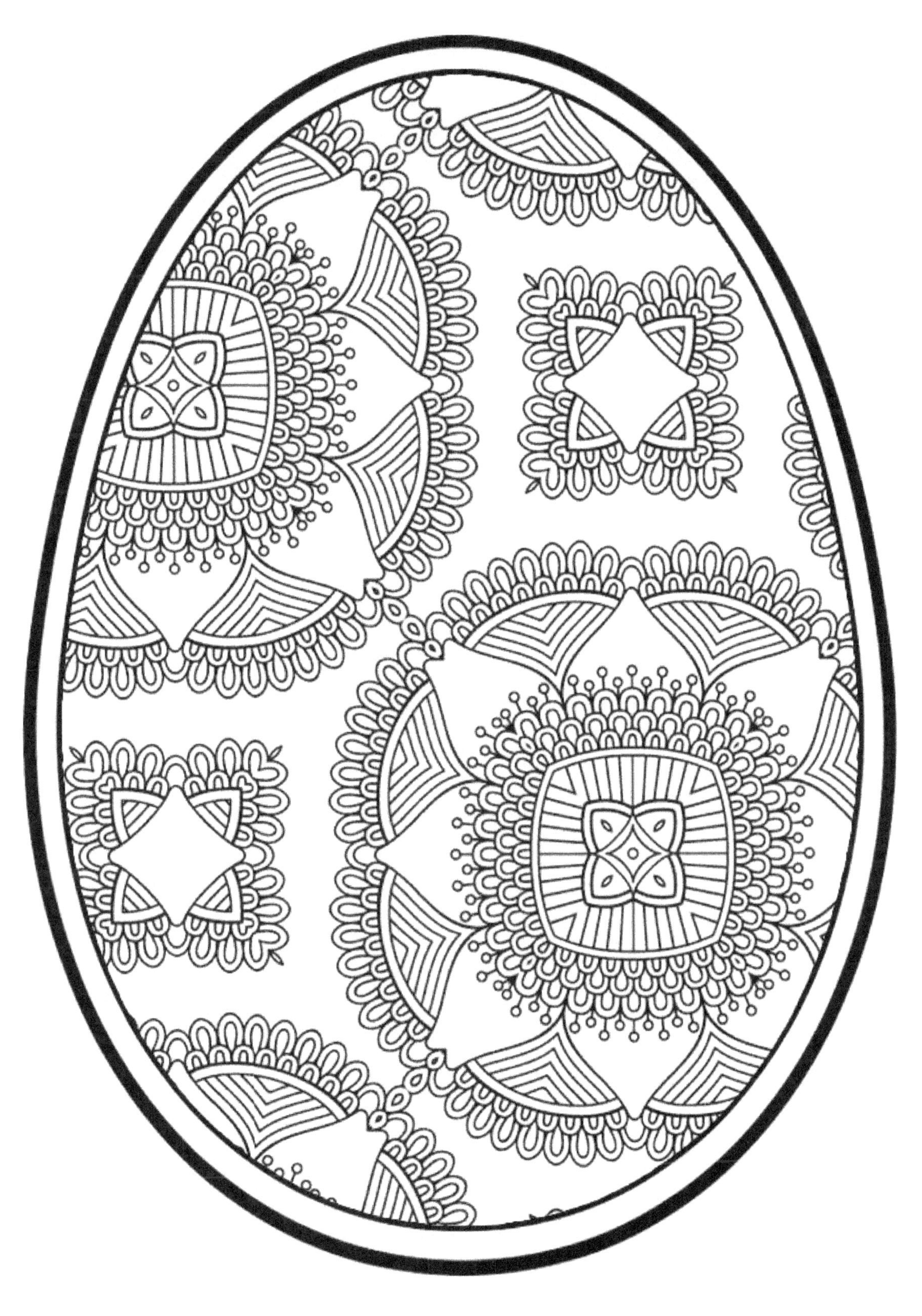

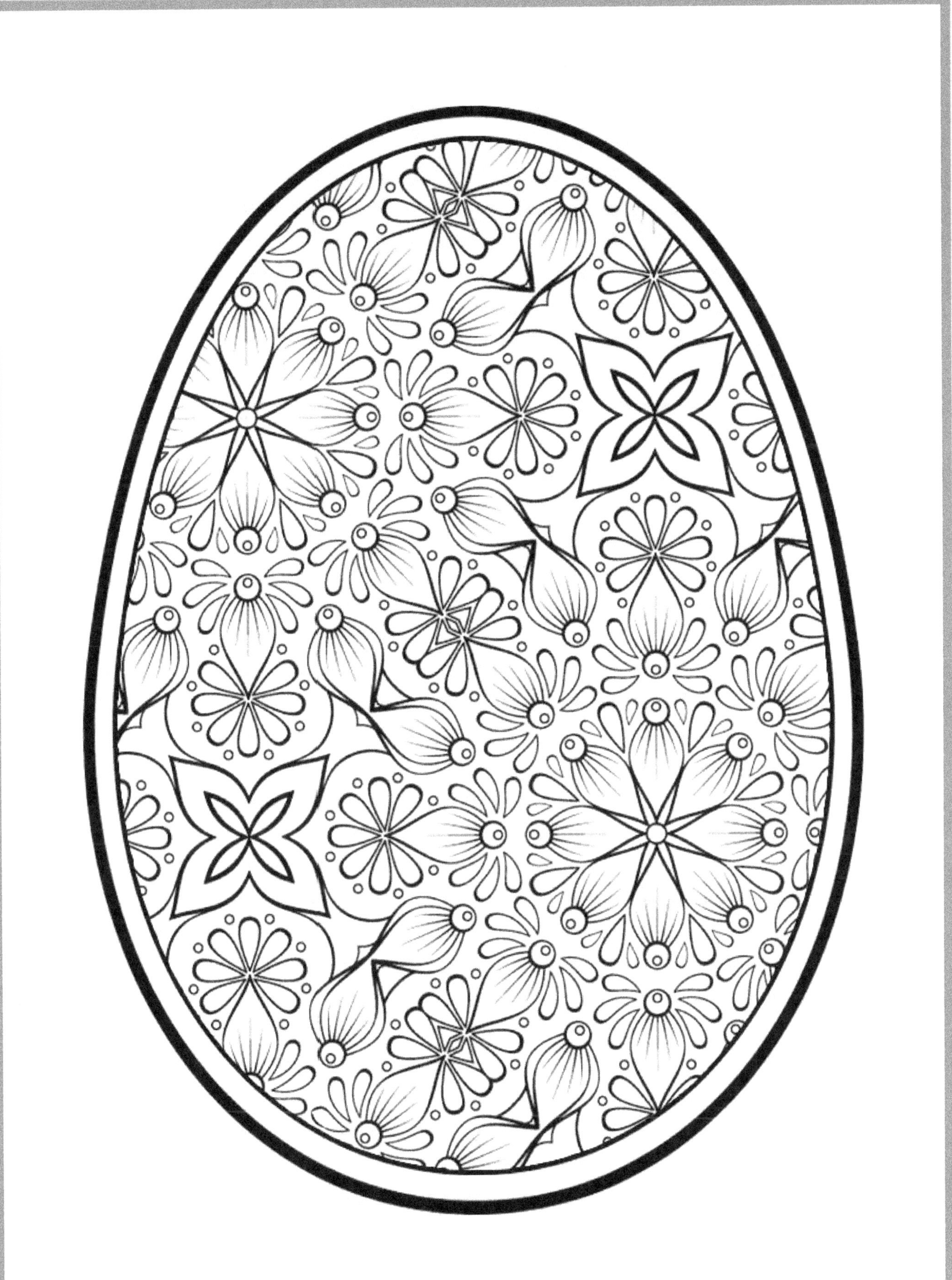

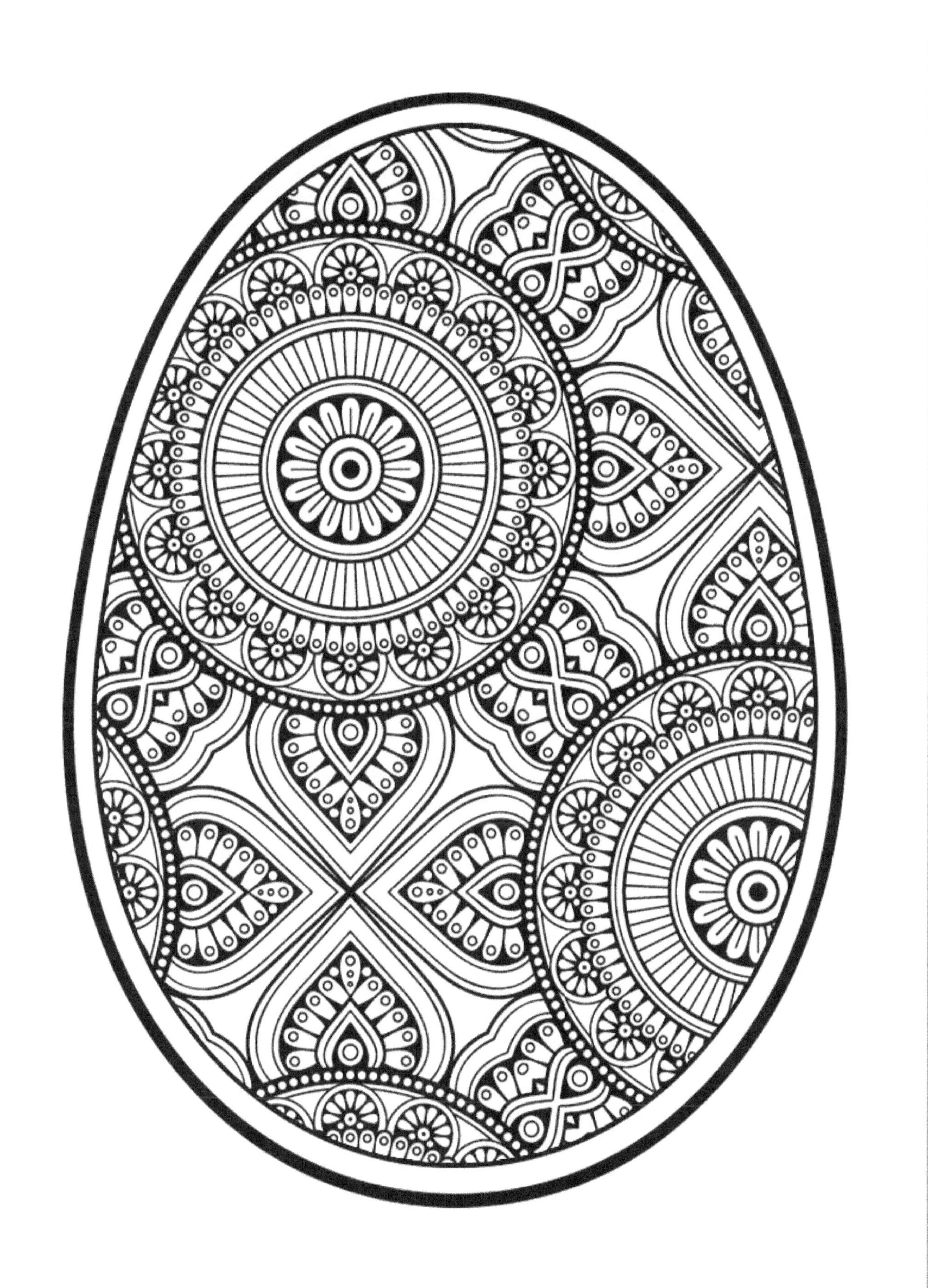

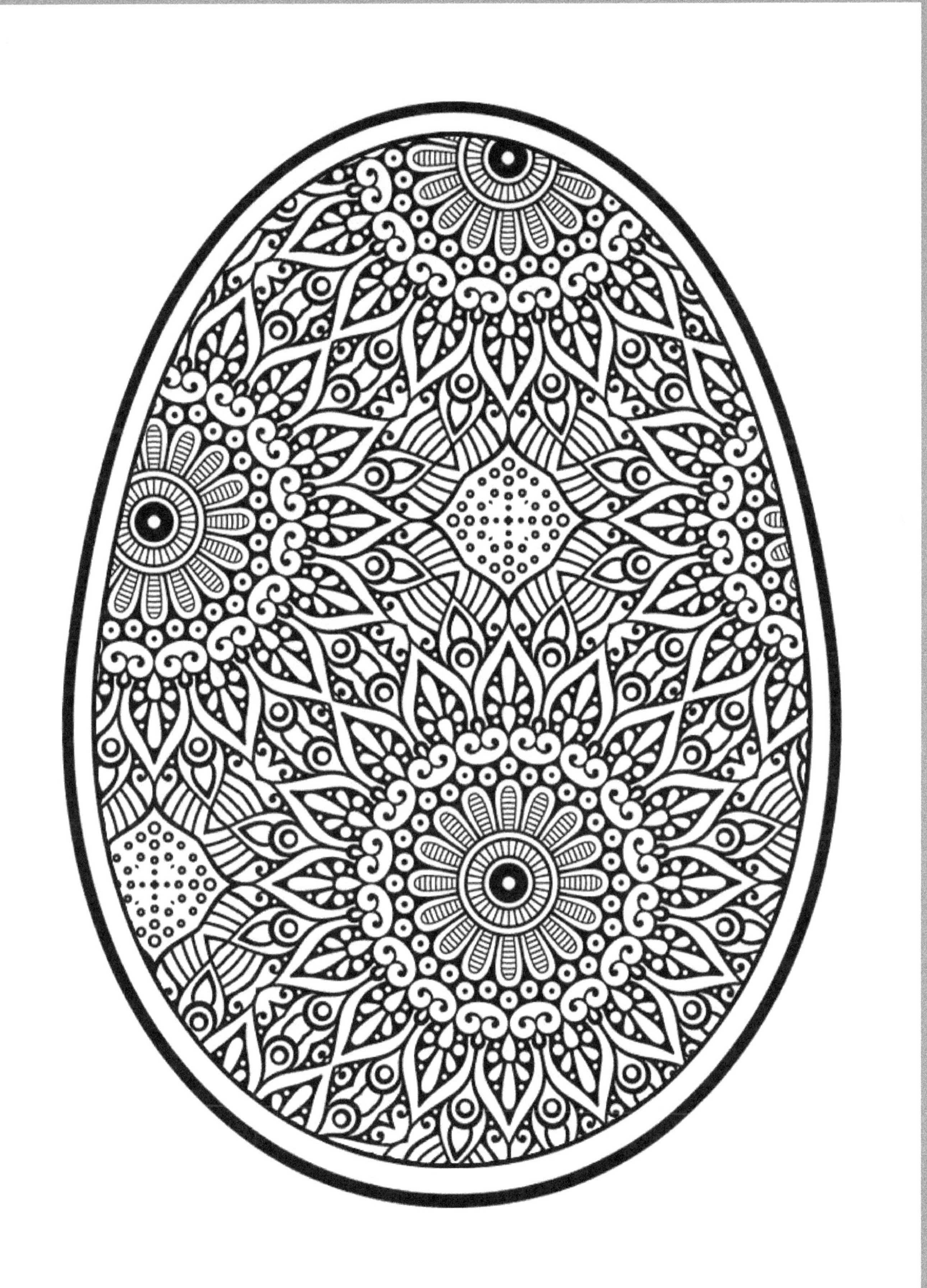

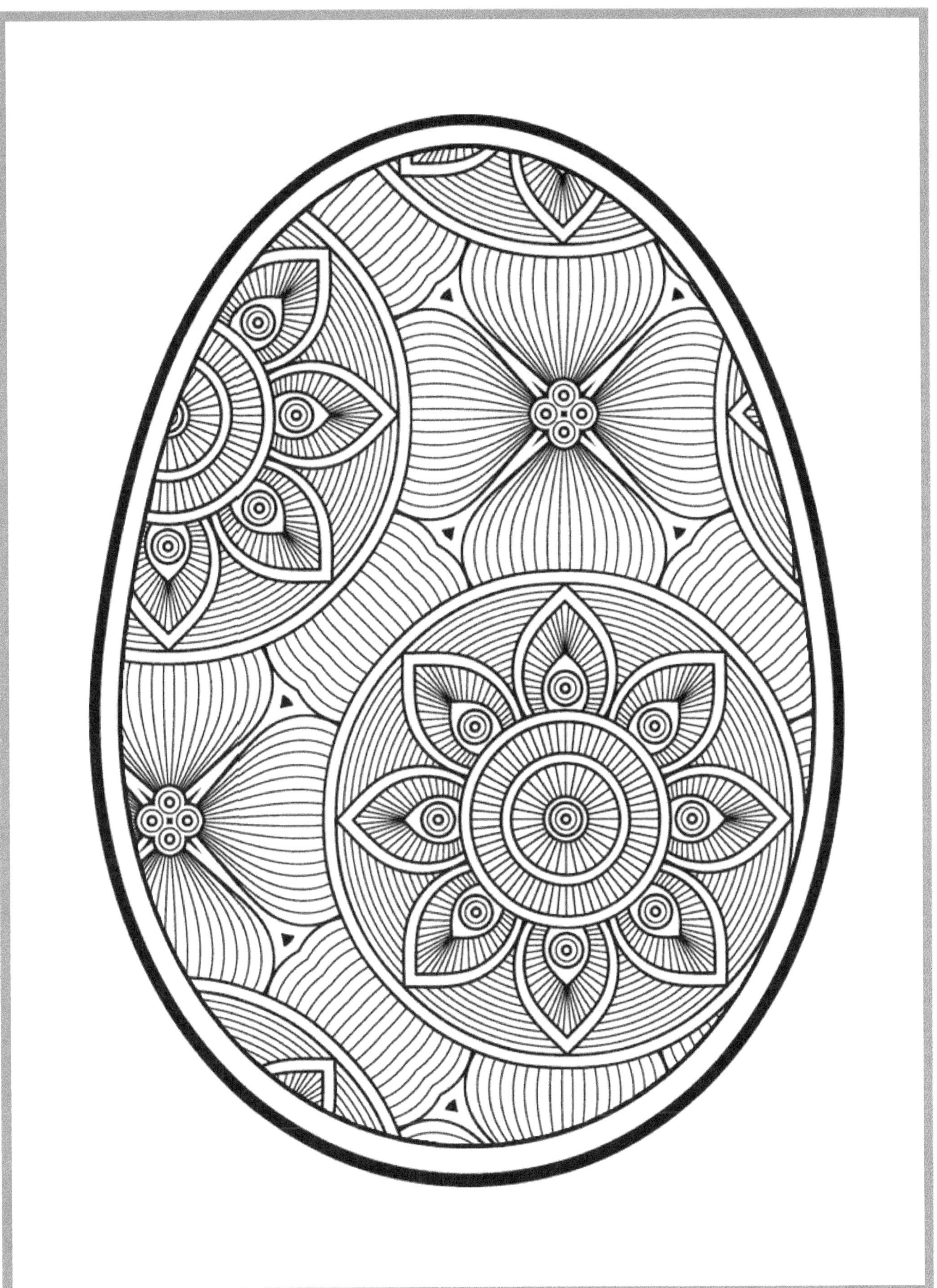

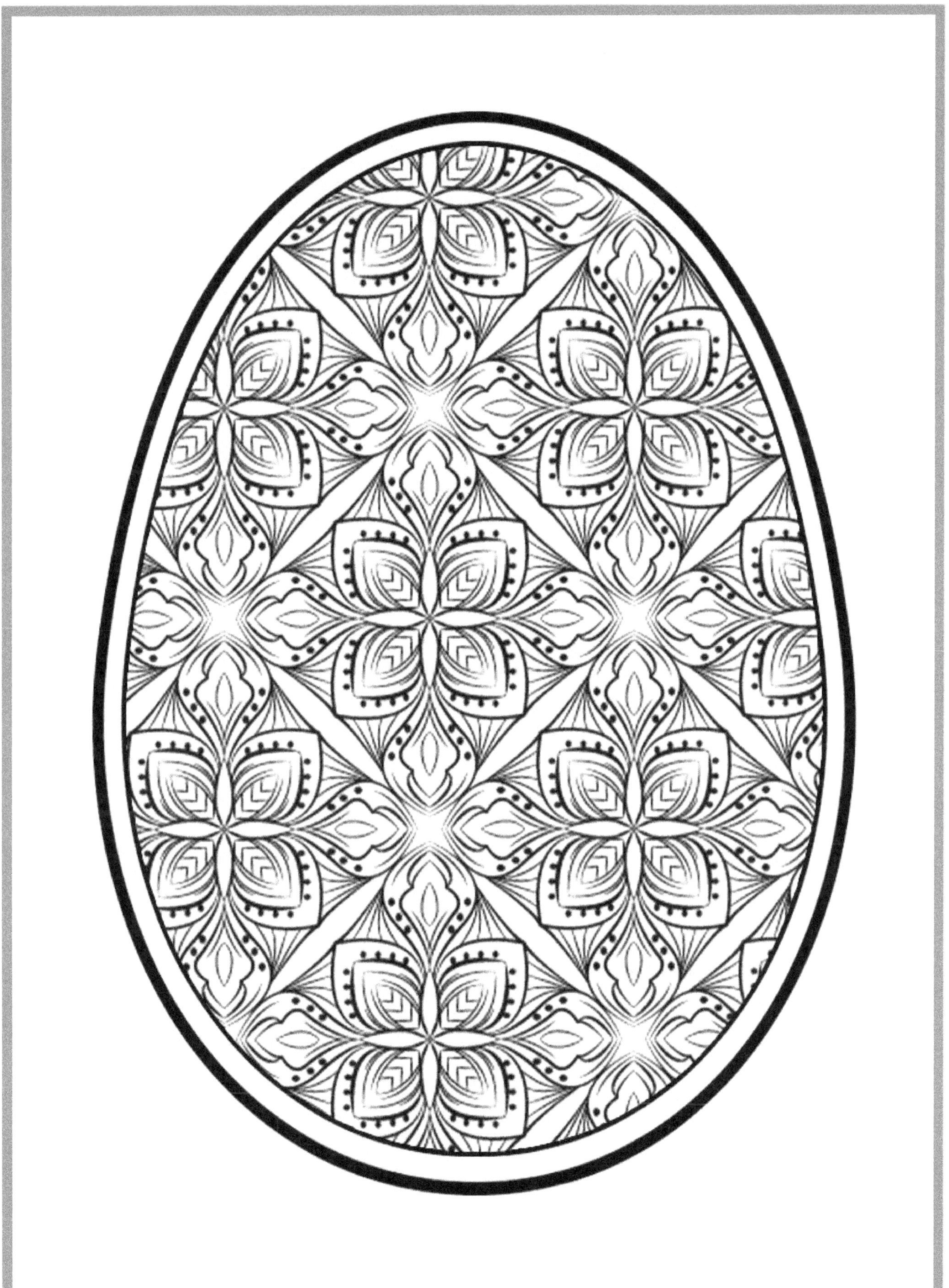

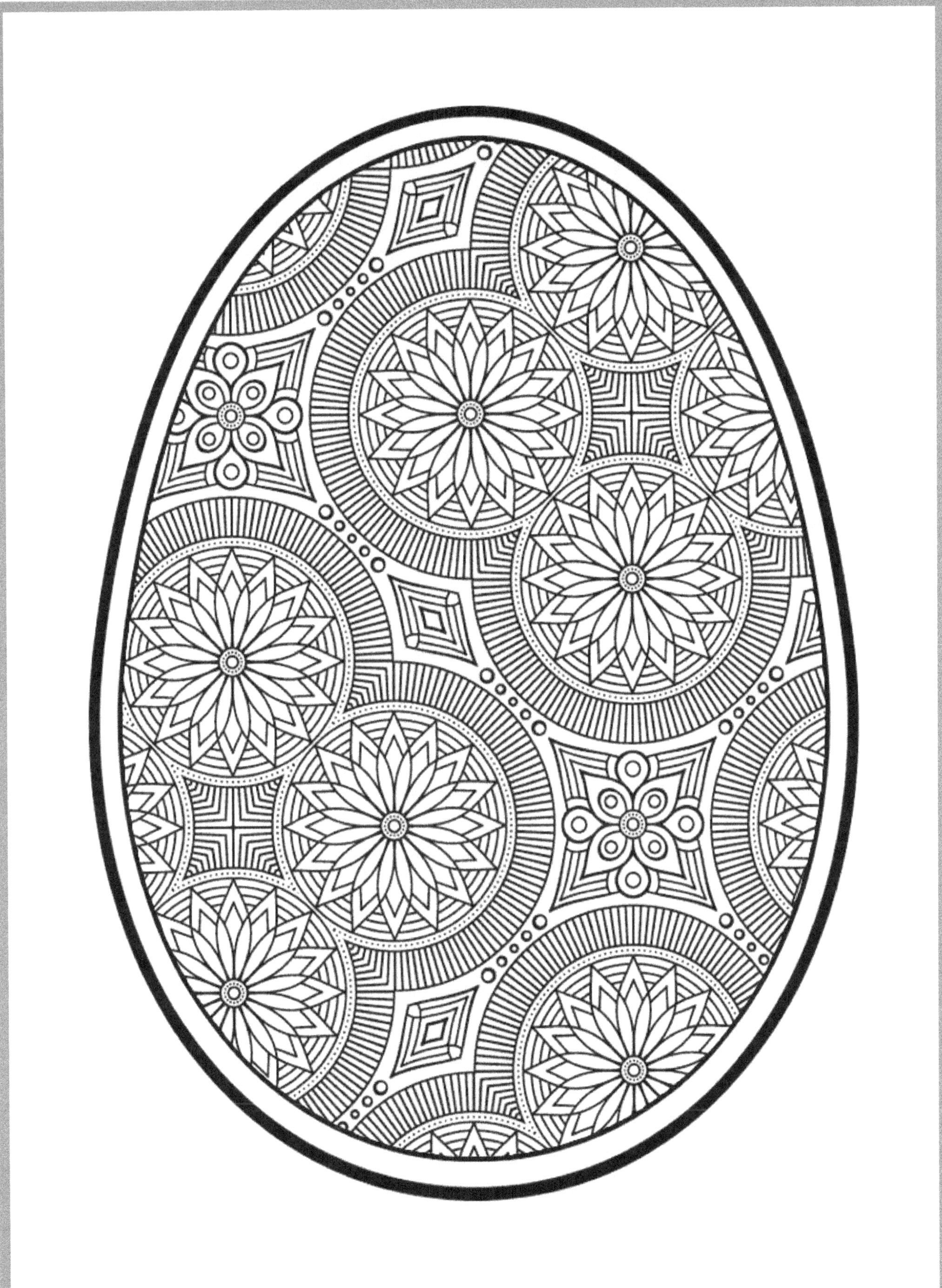

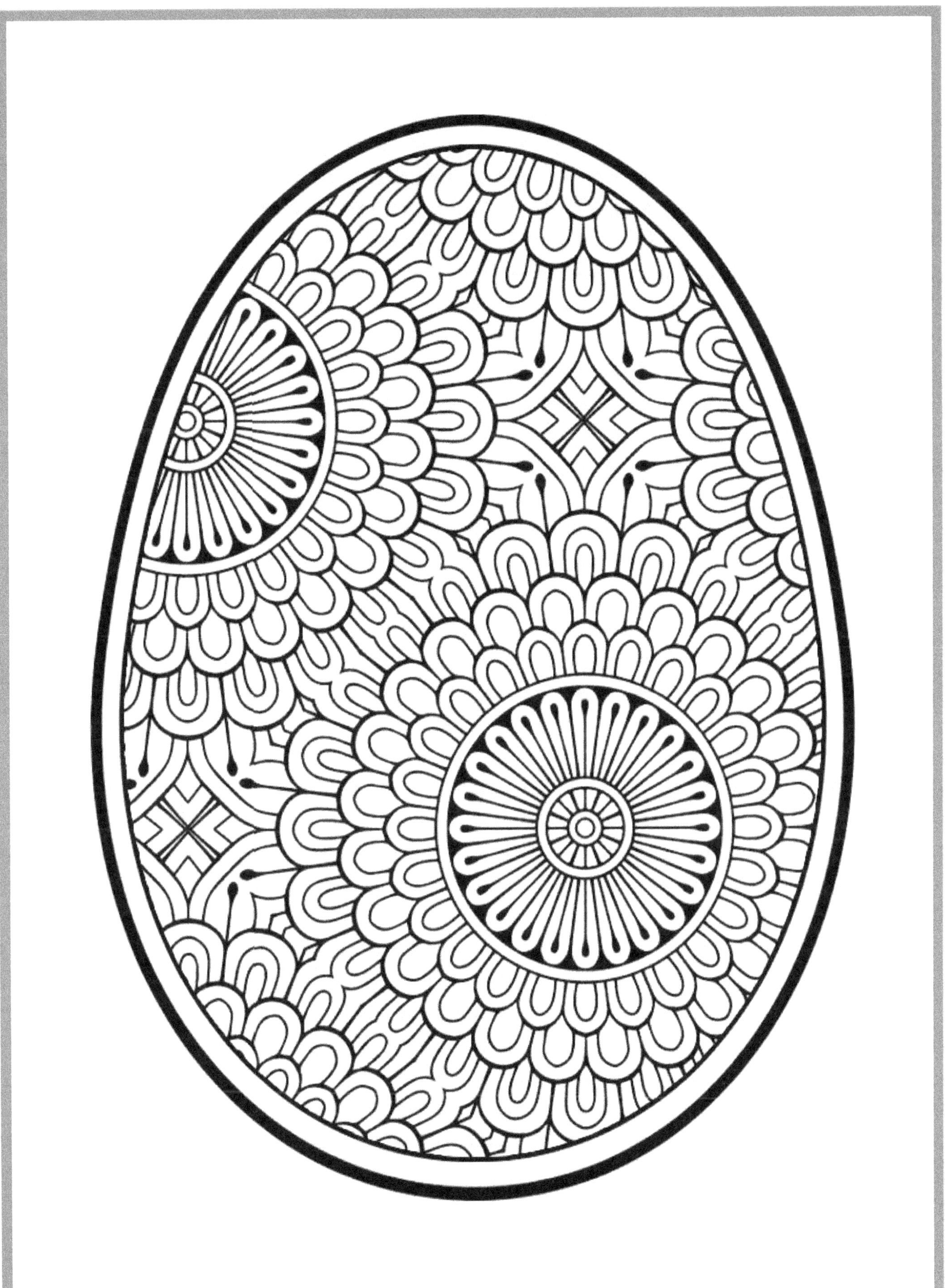

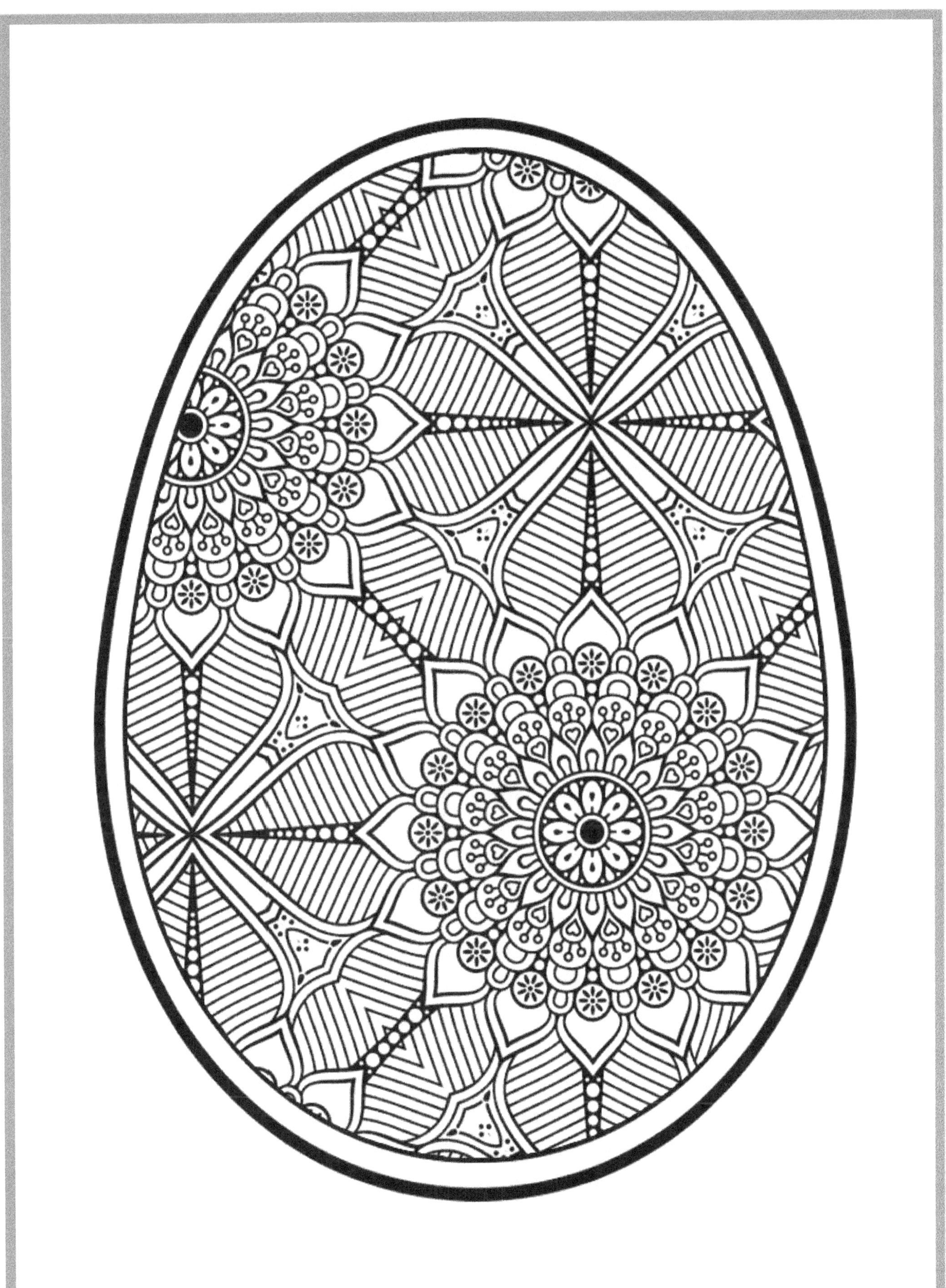

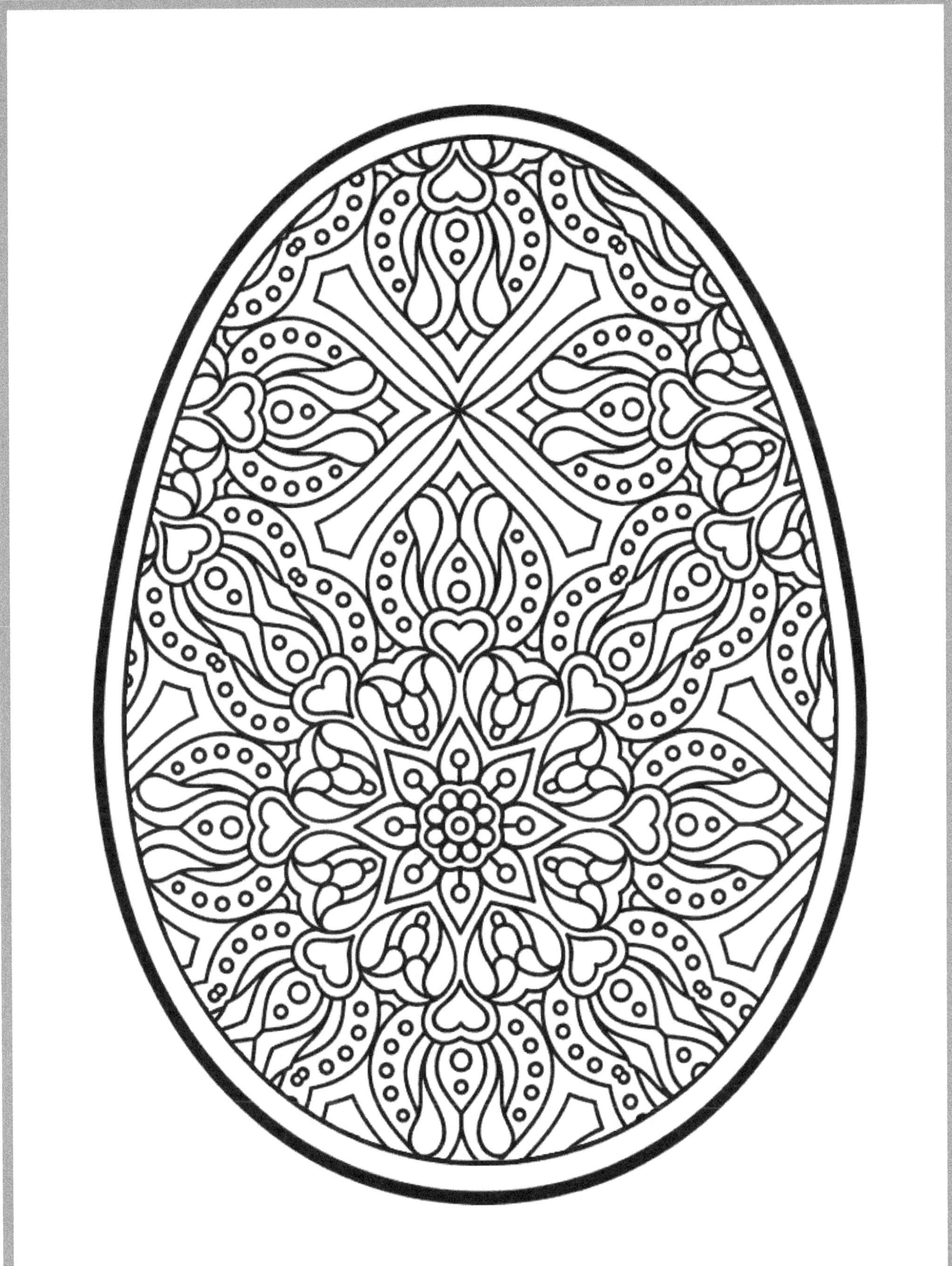

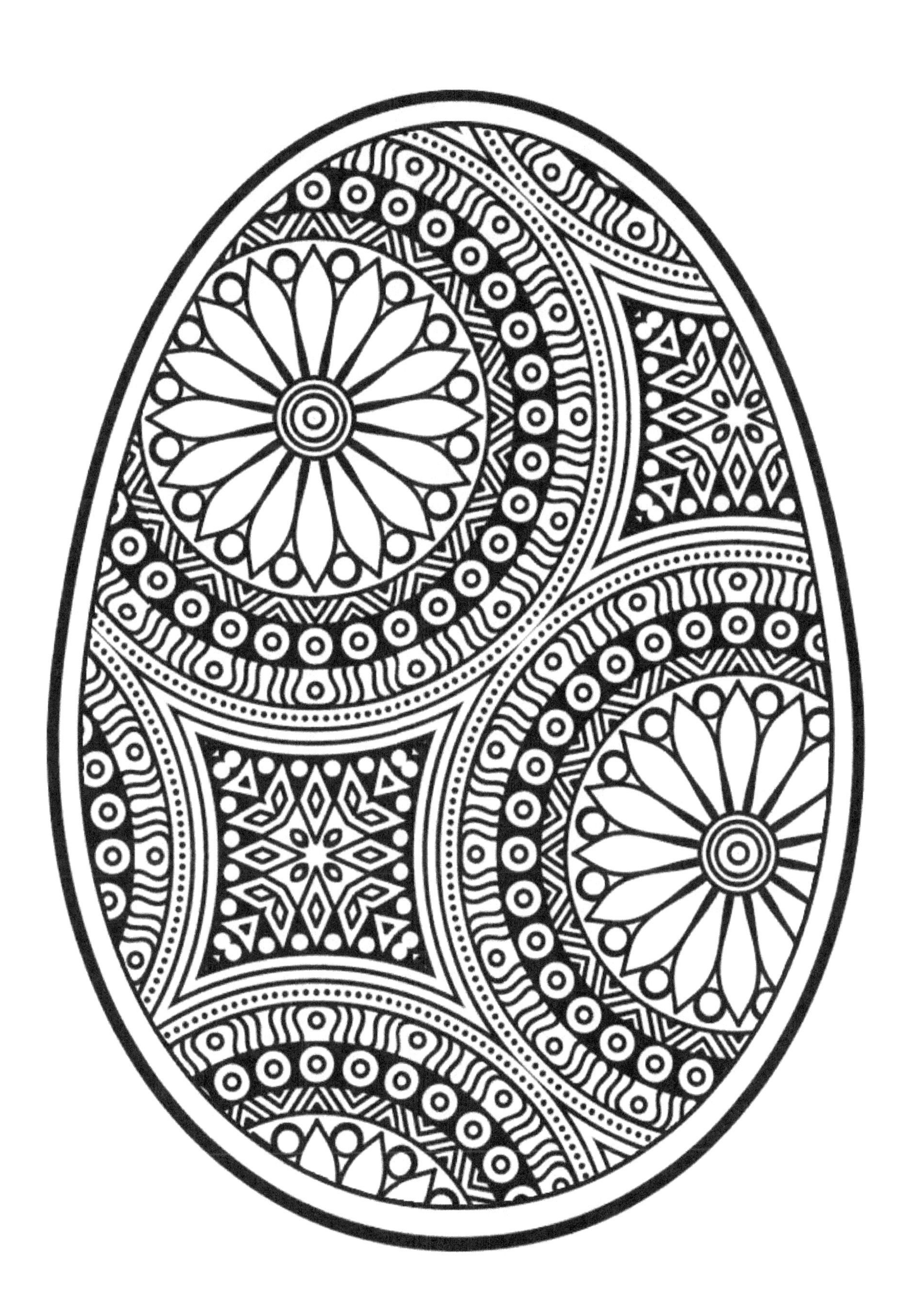

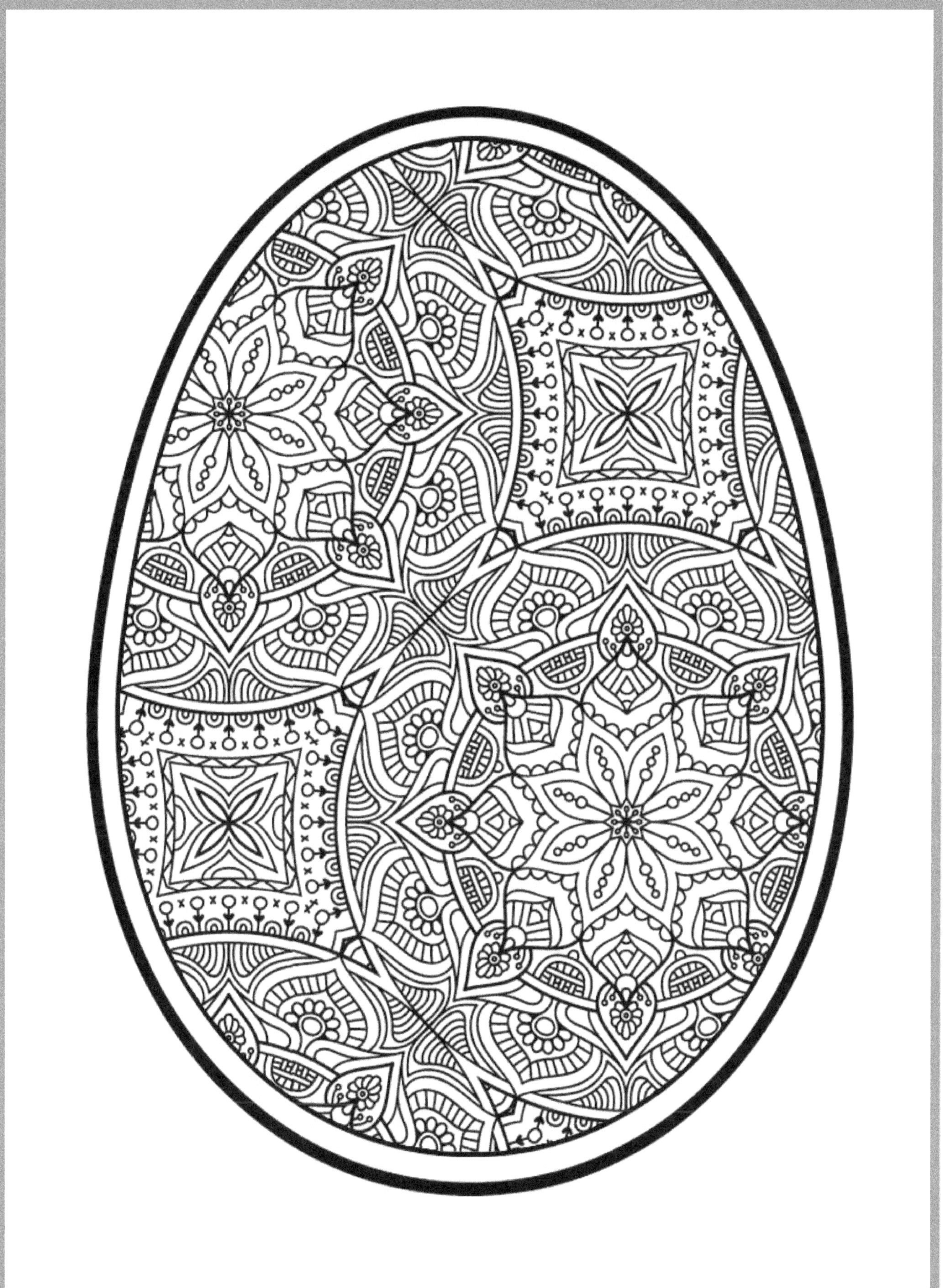

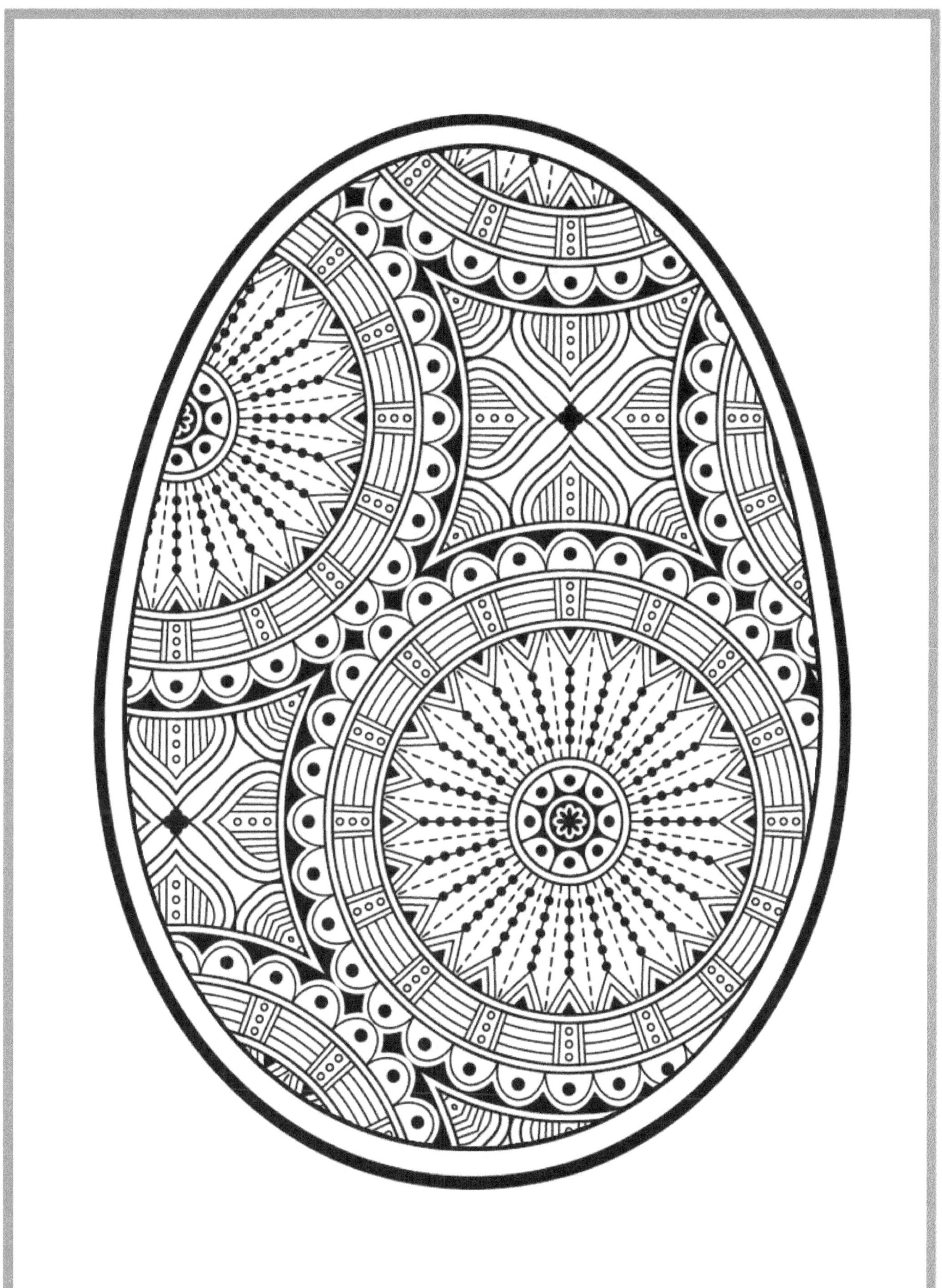

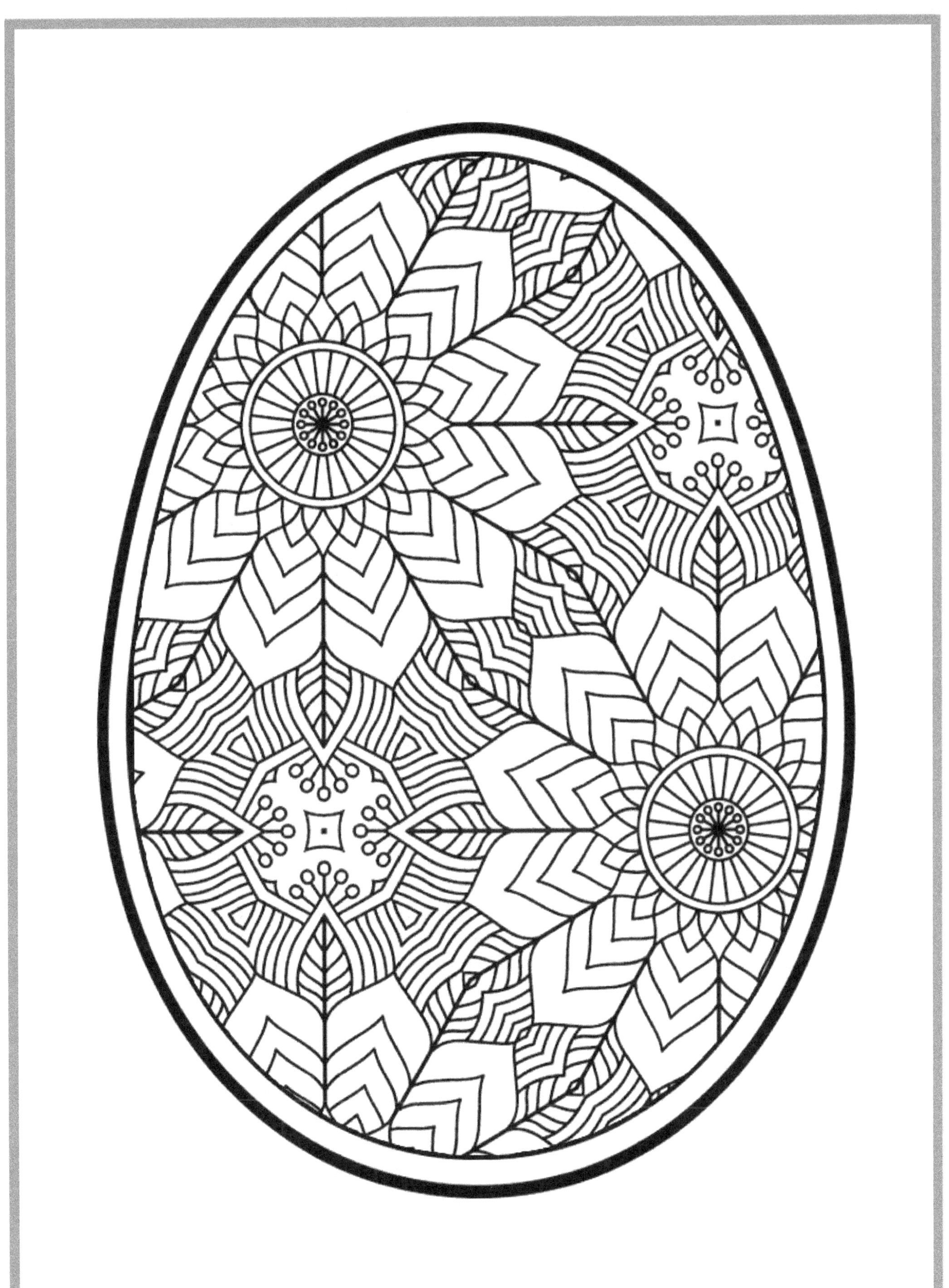

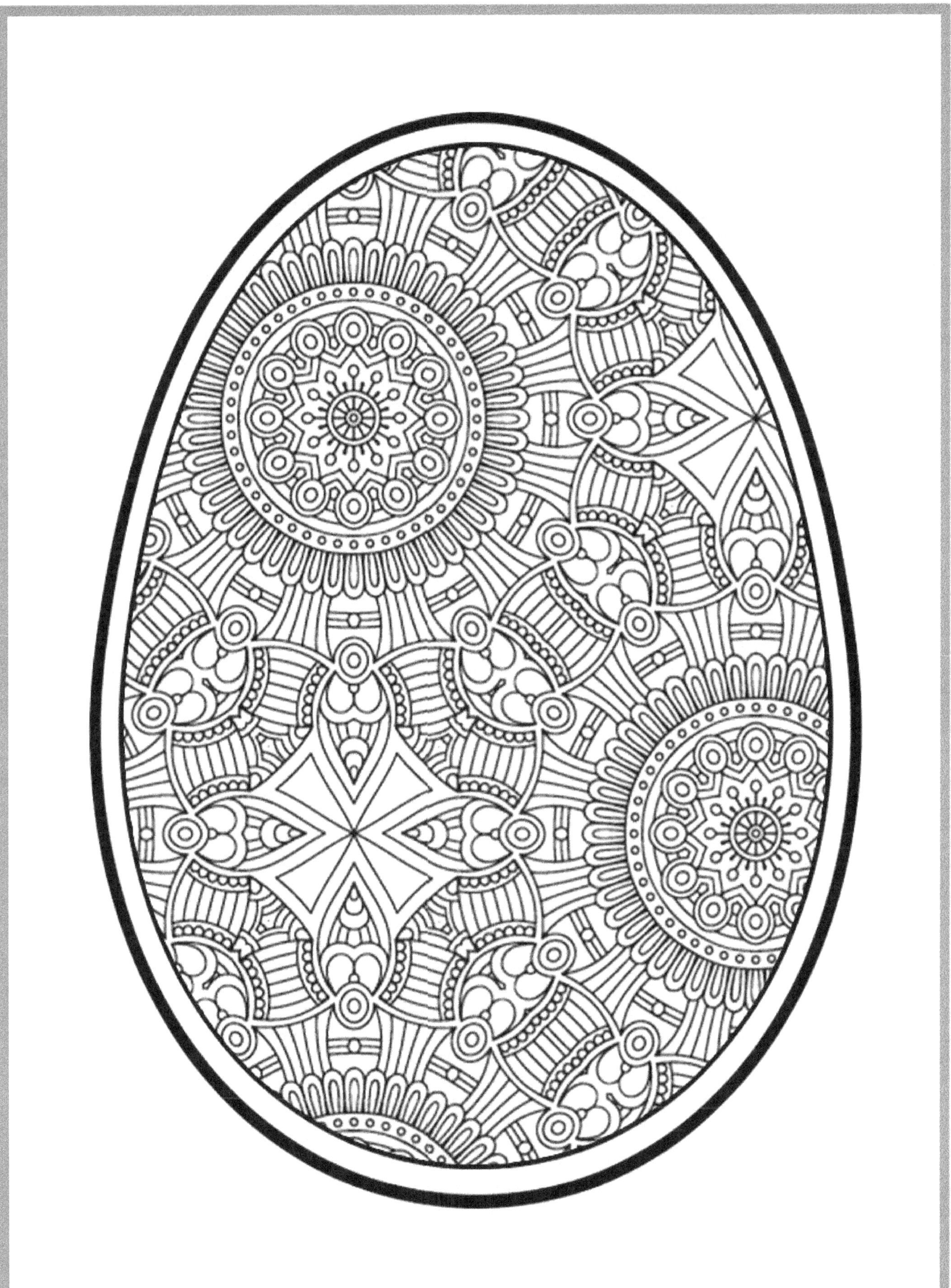

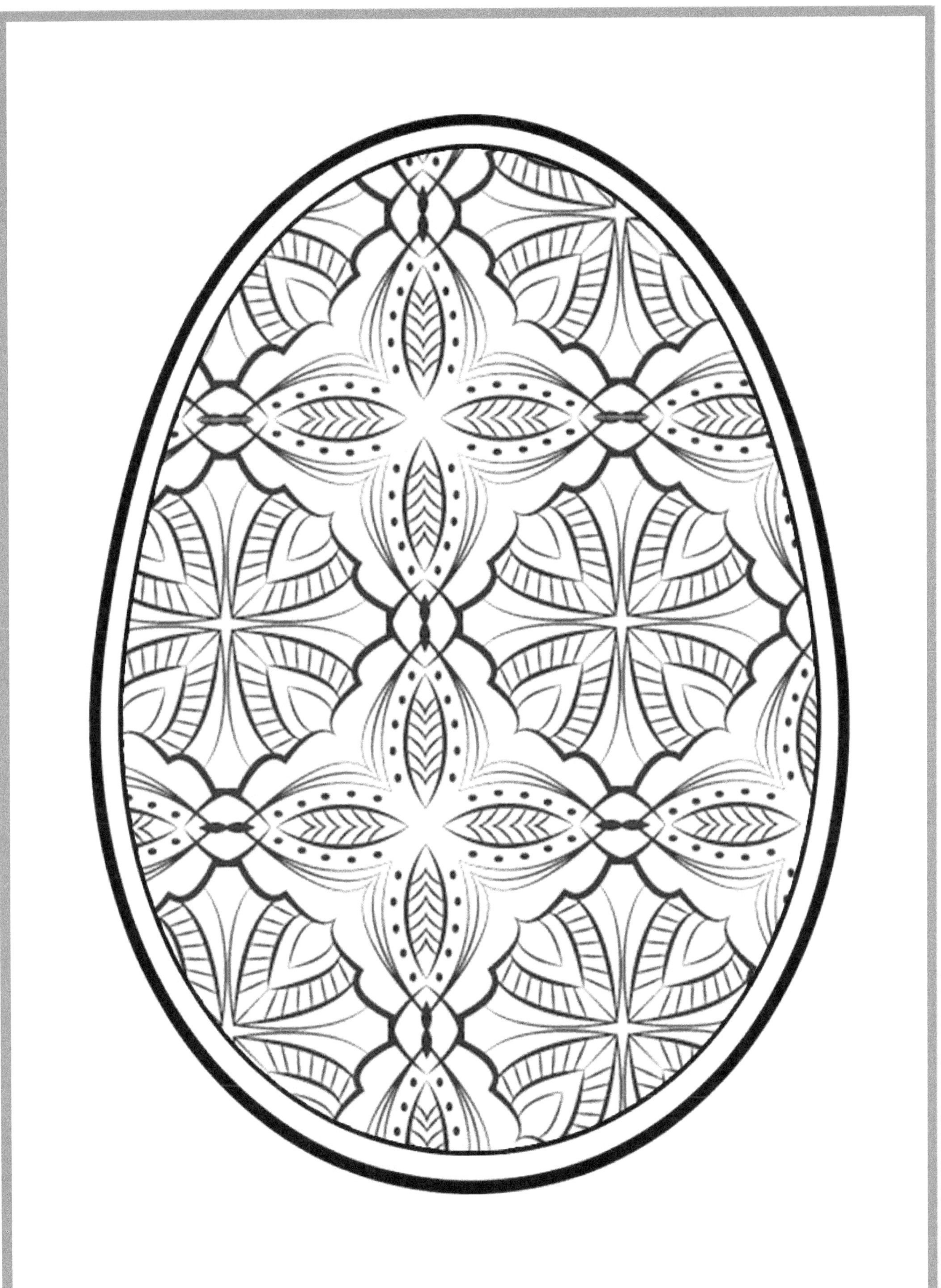